YOU CAN BE A WEDDING MC

*Everything you need to know
as a Master of Ceremonies
to ensure the reception
runs like clockwork*

Devised and written by Peter L. Miller

Second Edition

Praise for previous editions of YOU CAN BE A WEDDING MC

I found your book to be the best entrance into the world of a wedding MC; a complete and comprehensive guide to ensuring my clients special day ran smoothly and was memorable – I look forward to many years of being a wedding MC using your valuable tips and guides – a must have for all Comperes & MCs.
Simon Heart, Professional Magician, Gold Coast Queensland
simonheart1@aol.com

Just wanted to drop you a line and thank you for the terrific book 'YOU CAN BE A WEDDING MC'. As best man at my best mates wedding recently, I was also requested to perform the duties of the MC. When I was asked to do this, I accepted without thought of what this job actually entailed. As the date grew closer I began to become concerned due to the fact that I had absolutely no idea what really went on at a wedding given I usually turn up and proceed to just PARTY!!

I searched out your book and with its guidance enabled my friends to have a superb night. I not only received compliments on my performance, but people actually told me they were taking notes – as they had similar things to do in the future.

I am accustomed to public speaking and as such this was not an issue – however the small amount of nerves which are always around before any performance were confidently hidden due to the fact that I knew exactly what I was going to say and when. The words I chose to use from the book for introductions and welcomes were so perfect – succinct yet special. Thanks again – I could not have done it without you.
Duncan Savage, Hot Ice Partners duncan.savage@hoticepartners.com.au

I just wanted to 'Thank you' once again on the fabulous book 'YOU CAN BE A WEDDING MC'. It truly has made a difference to my confidence and my approach to my personal goals. I am a Customer Service officer for an office supply retailer. Last week I had my first gig as a wedding MC and I am definitely looking at it as a healthy source of income. The book thoroughly covered all the questions and fears about being an MC; let alone public speaking. You truly are to be credited on a book which has changed my life. Thank you Peter and I wish you continued success for your re-print in the overseas market.
Yours Sincerely, Steven Degollacion steved_75@hotmail.com

I tracked down a copy of your book at Dymocks – Chatswood. The book helped a lot. I had read your other book UP FRONT AND IN CONTROL but I needed something more specific to weddings. I got the book just in time and it helped me modify my introduction to put more of the focus back on the wedding couple and the significance of the day, rather than focusing on being funny or entertaining, which is secondary. I was very happy with how the MC role turned out, and the humour ended up presenting itself naturally anyway.
Alex Manning A.Manning@ mosman.nsw.gov.au

Praise from a distributor / retailer:
Peter Miller's 'YOU CAN BE A WEDDING MC' book has been part of my product range for approximately 2 years. I've found that it sells very well – it effectively delivers what it promises and is the only book that targets the topic that I'm aware of. It's an excellent gift idea for anyone wanting to feel confident about acting as an MC.
Nadia Fullerton info@newlywed.com.au

Here is the photo of my niece in her role of Wedding MC. This book was very helpful for my nephew (the groom) and my niece (the MC) in assisting them to structure their speeches and toasts. My niece ended up delivering a very humorous speech and using your book as her 'prop' with many references to you and the book. The common phrase by the end of the wedding was 'my friend Peter says . . .'.

Dayle Grant daylegrant@optusnet.com.au

My original idea of a Wedding MC would have been a short path to disaster.

However, with your brilliant book I was able to develop and customise a running sheet that gave the Bride and Groom an event to meet all their expectations and exceed many. Your book allows the MC to work within a comprehensive structure but still be spontaneous.

Paul G Bailey Mindbenders Pty Ltd FIVE DOCK 2046 Phone: 0413 049 944

If you are likely to be asked to MC a friend's or relative's wedding, this is the book for you. For anyone who can 'string a couple of words together', there is always the prospect that a well meaning friend or relative will unexpectedly make that fateful request one day. This happened to me recently and, in no small part due to Peter's book, I was able to ensure that my friend's special day was memorable for all of the right reasons.

YOU CAN BE A WEDDING MC is easily digested and contains all of the necessary tips and practical guidance for a budding MC. Dare I say it; there are even examples of humour to ensure the wedding reception rolls along in good spirit.

I congratulate Peter for producing such a valuable reference tool and, in so doing, ensuring that many weddings do not become an unwitting funniest home video entrant. YOU CAN BE A WEDDING MC should form part of everyone's 'must have' reference library.

Brad Petley. Brisbane, Queensland b.petley@nationalretailassociation.com.au

If you have any comments, criticisms or MC experiences you would like to tell us about, then please send your email message to enquiries@compere.com.au.

First Published in 2000
This revised and expanded edition published in 2004

A CORPORATE COMPERE Pty Ltd
PO Box 6241
North Ryde 2113 NSW Australia
Ph: (61 2) 9888 7123 Fax: (61 2) 9878 8550
Email: enquiries@compere.com.au
Web: www.weddingmc.com.au
A.C.N. 083 458 520

National Library of Australia
Cataloguing-in-Publication entry:

Miller, Peter
You can be a wedding MC: Everything you need to know as a
master of ceremonies to ensure the reception runs like
clockwork.

2nd ed.
Bibliography
Includes index.
ISBN 0 9578014 3 2

1. Master of ceremonies – Australia – Handbooks, manuals, etc.
2. Weddings – Australia. I. Corporate Compere Pty. Ltd.
II. Title.

392.50994

Designed by Midland Typesetters
Edited by Sue Wagner
Cartoons by Tony Kentuck
Cover designed by Harry Hughes at Fresh Ideas
Typeset in New York Font by Midland Typesetters
Printed in Australia by Southwood Press P/L
Back cover photo courtesy of Photogenic Studios

Contents

Foreword

The continued success of the Ritz Carlton is built from a careful selection of the staff we hire and their attitude towards superior service. We all work very hard to be a cut above the rest. So does Peter Miller.

Naturally we are also very discriminating with the selection of our outside suppliers who offer their services to our valued clients. However, when it comes to weddings, we are pleased to recommend Peter Miller as our preferred Master of Ceremonies.

Peter has been providing our clients with a first class wedding MC Service for a while now and the feedback we receive is excellent from both our staff and the bride and grooms.

We would like to congratulate Peter on releasing his new publication and wish him well with its success.

Narelle Bailey
Director of Catering
The Ritz Carlton
(Now the Stamford Plaza)
Double Bay, NSW Australia
June 2000

Foreword II

Curzon Hall

Sydney's Elegant Function Centre & Restaurant

Thursday, July 24, 2003

TO WHOM IT MAY CONCERN

Peter Miller has supplied Curzon Hall with MC's of the highest standard. Those MC's include his staff and himself. Peter is exceptionally professional, polished and very reliable as a MC. He places his clients immediately at ease with his organised and calm manner, quickly allowing them to relax and enjoy their event.

Peter is very reliable, always punctual, well dressed and completely dependable to run each event as planned.

We have recommended Peter and will continue to do so, as we constantly gain positive client feedback and praise for his MC skills.

To discuss this further, please telephone me directly on 02 9887 1877.

Yours Sincerely,

Jacqui Czako
VENUE ADMINISTRATION MANAGER

53 Agincourt Road Marsfield NSW 2122 Tel 02 9887 1877 Fax 02 9888 2450 Email info@curzonhall.com.au Web www.curzonhall.com.au

vii

Acknowledgements & Thank You's

Unofficially, you are holding the fourth edition of this book. The first was produced as a series of about ten different A4 templates printed on coloured paper – originally only for my personal use. Upon request, I made up each one separately and sold them as detachable forms with individual explanations secured in a plastic folder.

The next edition was printed off my PC and then photocopied and comb-bound. The success of this second stage prompted me to get serious and design a proper cover and pay for the entire book to be typeset and professionally printed.

The task has always been a work in progress – but I think that this version will be hard to significantly improve upon; so there are no plans for a fifth! However, I am certain that this standard of publication is the only one of its kind in the world.

Since there is very little written on how to MC a wedding, nearly all the concepts, ideas and opinions are my own; written either on the job or late at night after returning home energised but finding the rest of my family asleep. These thoughts have been my late night companion and I offer them to you as a way forward in order to make any wedding succeed beyond expectations. They have rigorously stood the test of time and you can be completely confident of their application and appeal.

In fact, I will guarantee their application by offering to gladly refund the purchase price of this book if you are not completely satisfied.

I would like to express my gratitude to my wife and two children for their patience and understanding during the odd hours, vacant weekends and missed holidays while the writing process took its course. Admiration goes to John Clingan, Jeff Bruce, Wil Scarlet, Gary Simmons, Luke Hayes and Silvio Ofira for offering their advice on the text and describing some of the lessons they have learnt from being excellent MCs.

Besides acknowledging my own persistence and love of what I do, I am indebted to my friend Monette Lee for her valuable proofreading. Thanks also must go to Joel Sweeney for the kid's quotes and to all the bride and grooms, the venues and the professional photographers, videographers and DJs for their encouragement, support and belief in my abilities as an MC and compere.

The talent of Chris Breckwoldt must be recognised for his hand drawing of an MC in the spotlight (inspired by a photo of Frank Sinatra). And thanks to Dorelle and Andy for their non-religious blessing.

Lastly, I need to recognise the help of Mr Ron Tacchi from Speakers Network International who, besides co-authoring UP FRONT IN CONTROL with me, has been a constant source of information, support and work for many years. Go 'Super Tac'.

I recommend you join the SWAP clubs spread throughout Australia and New Zealand and also the National Speakers Association in your own country and continue to expand the cake for everyone to enjoy. As my friend Max Hitchins says: Good luck, good laugh, good life.

Regards Peter L. Miller

http://www.nationalspeakers.asn.au   http://www.swapaustralia.com.au

I dedicate this book to my two lovely daughters Michelle and Madeleine.
I guess one day I will be hiring a good MC for their weddings!

Preface

This book is meant for people who realise what a huge difference a good Master of Ceremony can make to a wedding reception.

You can be a bride, a groom or a guest. You can be a friend or a relative, a trained and qualified toastmaster or a professional public speaker. You can also be a venue manager – interested in total customer service.

It has been written so the contents can be used instantly and accessed quickly. All the valuable templates are easily located in the back half. Yet there is still ample information to supply the experienced MC with inspiration and new ideas.

The object of this handbook is to raise the standard of what the public expects when they go to a wedding. For too long, the public has had to suffer old-fashioned and ill-prepared masters of ceremony who also use the opportunity to take over the function and try and be its star attraction.

This has tarnished the work of some truly adept and creative people whose experience as wedding MCs has helped me to write this timely and important book. With this completely revised second edition, there can be no excuse for any more weddings not being handled with smooth confidence and deft control.

Through the instruction and guidance of this manual, we can all look forward to a higher quality of wedding reception, ultimately making the occasion even happier than it would normally be.

Guests often assume the MC is a staff member

Q: What is the origin of love?
A: Cupid kissed God and that got the ball rollin'.
                JULIO, AGE 9

A unique opportunity

There are not many times in your working life when you will share a loving, intimate moment in the life of your clients. However, for a wedding MC, these cherished scenes are part of the job description! Because of this consistently unique chance, the job of a wedding MC is nearly always a privilege to perform.

Wedding MCs help create an image of lasting happiness. The memories that two people will carry with them for the rest of their lives will be influenced by the work of the MC and all the other professionals working on their wedding day. There are few industries that operate in such caring conditions and boast such a loving environment.

As an example of the powerful emotional nature of this event, I can vividly remember many more wedding receptions than I can recall memories of corporate MC jobs. This is because love leaves enduring traces upon the human heart – memories of love, linger long after the event has faded.

Making an impression

The guests do not want an MC who is there to steal the limelight. Their friends are the bride and groom, and they want the MC to show that he or she appreciates this by showing deference and creating a sense of intimacy and sexiness.

The memory of a wedding reception will always contain a comment about what the MC was like. This might be the very first time that many of the guests have witnessed a good MC in action, and they are often astonished to discover the difference this professionalism can make to the overall success of a function.

A large part of the responsibility for creating this success falls to the MC. There are many and varied duties to perform, one of which is making a collection of people from different origins and age groups, who are there for different reasons, feel comfortable enough to let their hair down and rejoice. The individual guests will often know only a very small group of people, and they may have little in common with each other, apart from knowing the bride and groom.

This eclectic combination of people makes a wedding reception a special challenge for an MC to gauge. They can range from young pageboys and flower girls to elderly matriarchs and patriarchs; from work acquaintances to school day buddies and from long-time neighbours to personal friends of the parents.

(Even though they share many similarities in preparation, a wedding is nothing like a normal business function where people are often forced to attend and all know each other socially.)

Everyone at a wedding loves the free drinks and may be tempted to celebrate wildly, but at the same time they do not wish to accidentally offend or embarrass the bride and groom on their special day. The children will be desperate to slide along the polished shiny dance floor, but their parents will forbid it because they have just spent half a week's wages on their child's first formal outfit.

At the same time, at least half of the group will be feeling emotional because a new personal threshold has been reached. Friendship will be redefined forever when the bride and groom depart at the end of the reception. It behoves the MC to bring this nervous group of partygoers together and point them in the right direction.

Throughout the event, the MC must continually adapt to the changing energy and happiness levels of the bride, the groom and the guests. The graph below shows how a wedding reception might feel to a guest if the speeches were after the main course.

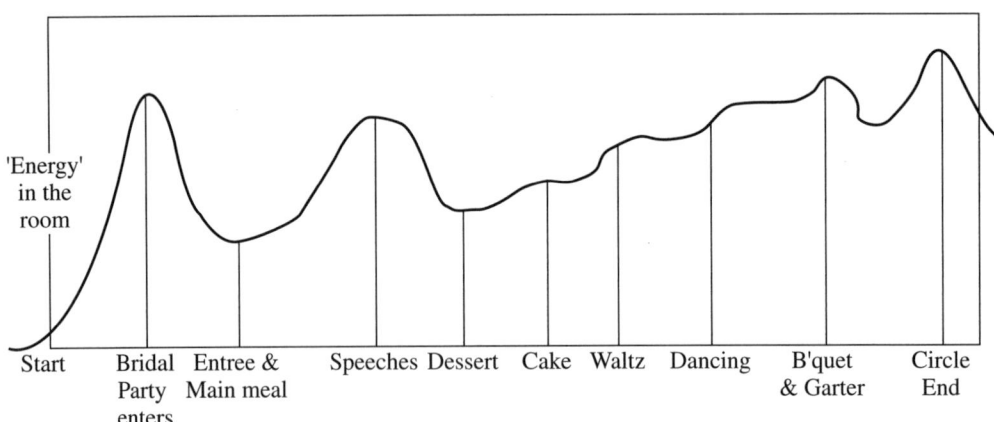

Energy levels at a wedding reception

The wedding reception is unique in that it is an extended celebration that can last up to seven or eight hours. Therefore, besides everything else the MC does, he or she has to ensure that the high points are spaced out and do not fall together at one time. The MC can monitor the ebb and flow of the event and thus give everyone time to recover and get ready for the next crescendo. You can refer to the MC's CHECKLIST for a more detailed sequence.

Responsibilities

The MC can become the bride and grooms closest ally. They can rely on their MC to help them throughout the potentially stressful and often tiring reception. The MC enters the wedding reception fresh and energised, while the bridal party has already posed for hundreds of photographs, stood through a religious ceremony and sometimes even battled extreme weather conditions.

Before reaching the reception venue, the guests have also attended the marriage ceremony, either in a church or a setting of serene and natural beauty. Arriving at the reception, they are looking for a way to alter the restrained mood and relax; the MC provides that way. The main thing to keep in mind is that people are there to underline celebrate because two people have fallen in love and have chosen this day to tell the world about it. This public declaration is a very happy occasion, despite all the cynics and comedians doing their best to make it seem like a prison sentence!

Weddings are conventional but friendly events, filled with an atmosphere of 'love' – a word the wedding MC should not be afraid to use during the night. As in any form of public speaking, it is important to use words that are appropriate to the theme of the event. However, it is easy to allow these well-meaning words fall into the realm of cliché. Use them when the time feels suitable; in other words, when you are personally inspired too.

Thinking creatively

The dearest wish of every bride and groom when they are planning their wedding is to make their reception unique, individual and memorable. This can be achieved by thinking of a theme that suits their personality.

My wife and I managed to achieve this 'memorability' at our wedding reception by having a theme of 'Colour' for the dress-code. It immediately put the guests in the mood for some fun. Added to this, the MC was my brother-in-law Jeff Bruce. He sang a few songs at the conclusion of the speeches. Not to be out-done, the best man (Chris Breckwoldt) and I broke the rules by removing our ties and jackets, and adopted a different 'night club' look with darker coats. We then proceeded to serenade the bride and groom's mothers with long-stemmed roses as we sang 'Spanish Harlem' and '(Sittin' on the) Dock of the Bay'. Chris had never sung in public before!

However, what really brought the house down was when the bride appeared in a fresh gown, grabbed the microphone and sang up a storm with her new husband. Three duets later, the guests were ready to really go wild. It took a lot of effort and courage to do that (some might even say stupidity) but the guests still talk about it today, some fifteen years later.

Another creative outlet is to give each table a name instead of a number. This can save the embarassing 'pecking order' routine while the names can be based around the favourite activities of the couple. For instance, one couple were very keen snow skiers so they named each table after well-known ski resorts.

The system

Weddings are a steady source of work for MCs and provide opportunities to learn the trade and sharpen their skills. Because of this consistency (and a lower fee scale than for corporate work) there might be a temptation to treat the wedding reception as a simple procedure and not a function that requires the same groundwork as a special one-off event might need.

To counter this potential problem, I have created a 'system' using a series of templates. This means the MC can give an impression of professionalism and use their time effectively and efficiently. This format has been refined over several years and tested at hundreds of receptions, by many different MCs. The system gives the MC a solid structure to start with but allows them to be flexible in the way they apply it.

I have made it easy to find these <u>templates</u> by slotting them in at the back of the book. Each template has its own 'explanation' on the page before it.

Q. How does a person learn to kiss?
A: You learn it right on the spot when the gushy feelings get the best of you.
BRIAN, AGE 7

Some form of celebration of marriage has been making the world turn since the dawn of time. This strong sense of tradition is both a help and a hindrance to the MC. In this book, I hope to cover every aspect of a traditional wedding celebration that an MC might expect to encounter.

Ethnic weddings

In every country, there are extremely strong <u>traditions</u> relating to wedding receptions; and especially in the role of a master of ceremony.

It is important for every bride and groom to know that their guests are comfortable and feel relaxed. A native-speaking person 'up front' at a wedding reception (that involves people of different ethnic origins) will really help to achieve this. A multilingual MC will reassure the bride and groom's parents and their friends, and make everyone feel as though the couple are taking at least some of the old traditional values with them into their marriage.

Many MCs find extensive work opportunities throughout the ethnic communities if they can speak a second language. Nevertheless, there is still work inside a multicultural society for MCs who are good at their job but only speak English.

A quick 'Good evening' in the appropriate language could be sufficient to cross cultural boundaries. You might like to use the following (some are written phonetically) to break the ice:

Armenian	Bar ree yeah rare go
Croatian	Dobra vet chay

Czech	Dobri dan
Filipino	Cum ma star
French	Bonjour
German	Guten arpen
Greek	Carlee sperrah suss
Italian	Bwona sera
Japanese	Con knee chi wah
Macedonian	Tra bel
Maltese	Kar fin tee
Polish	Dobra veit trude
Spanish	Buenas not chess
Vietnamese	Chao quan cut

All of these roughly translate as good evening and welcome.

Good humour, enthusiasm and talent
are understood by everyone.

A popular European tradition is the eating of bread and salt upon the entrance of the bride and groom. This is given by their parents in front of the bridal table (before they sit). These two 'necessities of life' are meant to ensure that the couple never go hungry (the bread) or are never poor (the salt; which was once more valuable than gold).

You might also experience the smashing of a plate – which the groom has to sweep up; and remind the couple that the toilet has to be flushed before midnight wherever they are staying for the evening.

Some traditions require the bride and groom to be the last remaining people at their reception. This might be necessary if the couple are going to accept envelopes of money from their guests at the conclusion of the event. The envelope 'gift' is a great European, Middle Eastern and Asian wedding reception tradition. The gifts may amount to tens of thousands of dollars, which can give the couple a good financial start.

Naturally there needs to be someone trustworthy charged to collect all this money. This is usually one of the parents of the bride and groom who have sometimes made up a special 'letter box' that makes it easy to safely deposit the envelope through.

One of the features of a Greek wedding reception is when the bride gets money pinned to her dress. Lebanese parents of a bride and groom tend to give gold jewellery because they feel it is more personal than cash.

These traditions serve a very good purpose which unfortunately is sadly lacking in Western celebrations, when, at the conclusion of the wedding reception, the bride and groom start their married life together with a huge debt to repay! One way this tradition could be introduced into our commemorations of marriage is for the bride and groom to make it clear in their invitation that they would prefer cash to gifts, rather like the 'red envelopes' of Chinese New Year.

A further extension of this custom is that many guests look at the donation of cash as a personal loan. This theory says that the same amount is due in return if the giver gets married or ever gets into financial trouble.

Another sweet tradition is the 'Wishing Well'. This involves a wooden structure set up so the guests can make a wish and then donate some cash into the 'well' to help the bride and groom on their way.

'I wish you 100 years of happiness'   TRADITIONAL VIETNAMESE WEDDING BLESSING

Be careful how you handle a speech spoken in another language. Many of the audience might be feeling alienated because they did not understand a single word during the last couple of minutes. To make matters worse, if the speech was either funny or incredibly touching, half the audience will be in a different frame of mind and the other half will not know why. To diffuse this potentially uncomfortable situation, I have found that a simple statement such as *'Well, I don't speak Italian, but I agree with everything he said'* brings everyone back to the same level again. On the other hand, an English translation or interpretation of a speech by one of the guests might be most welcome. This is something to discuss with the bride and groom in advance so it can be organised.

How to say 'I Love You' in many different languages
Albanian...................Une Te Dua
Arabic ....Ana Bhibbik
Catalan ....Testimo Molt
Chinese ....Wo Ai Ni
Eskimo ....Nagligivaget
Finnish ....Mina Rakkastan Sinua
French ....Je T'aime
German ....Ich Liebe Dich
Greek.......................S'Agapo
Hawaiian ....Aloha Wau la Oe
Hebrew......................Ani Ohev Otakh
Hungarian ....Se Ret Lay
Irish ....Thaim In Grabh Leat
Italian ....Ti Amo
Japanese ....Ai Shite Imasu
Maltese.....................ien Inhobbok
Persian.....................Du Stet Daram
Redneck ....Nice Tits
Romanian ....Te iubesc
Russian.....................Ya Lyublyu Tyebya

Spanish.....................Te Amo
Swedish....................Jag Alskar Dig
Turkish ....Seni Seviyorum

Anniversaries

With all the tragic figures of divorce rates climbing, it is a great inspiration to the bride and groom to be reminded that there are shining examples of happy marriages sometimes found as a rich gem inside their own guest list. This question on the INTERVIEW sheet serves to jog the memory of both the MC and the couple to make mention of these wonderful anniversaries at some time during the reception; usually at the opening introductions or during the speeches.

These milestones are significant and each year has its own particular symbol that serves as a suggestion for a gift.

1st year	paper	13th year	lace
2nd year	cotton	14th year	ivory
3rd year	leather	15th year	crystal
4th year	flowers	20th year	china
5th year	wood	25th year	silver
6th year	sugar	30th year	pearl
7th year	wool	35th year	coral, jade
8th year	bronze	40th year	ruby
9th year	pottery	45th year	sapphire
10th year	tin, aluminium	50th year	gold
11th year	steel	55th year	emerald
12th year	silk	60th year	diamond

If one of the guests is celebrating a birthday, leave the announcement until the Circle; or at least until the end. This way, the occasion will still be recognised and celebrated but will not take focus from the real guests of honour.

Introducing entertainers

Since it's a one-off event that will obviously never happen again, the bride and groom should spend as much time with their guests as humanly possible. The MC works for this to happen smoothly. Therefore, I find it hard to justify the value of separate entertainers at a wedding reception, even though I come from a background in entertainment. (Please do not confuse this comment with the need for a dance band; good dance music is absolutely essential, and there can be nothing better than the live variety.)

Some traditions require individual entertainment at a wedding reception and so it must be ordered. If the speeches are after main course, the best spot for the entertainment is after entrée. Often the performers will not be full-time, working professionals and may need guidance to give a trouble-free show.

After their change rooms have been organised, the MC should ask the entertainers the following list of questions:

- How do you want to be introduced?
- How long is your show?
- How many songs?
- How will I know it is the last song?
- Do you perform an encore if the crowd wants one?
- Do you involve the bridal party?
- Can I give your music to the DJ, or would you rather speak to them personally?
- Would you like some drinks?
- Have you been paid beforehand or are you collecting your fee now?

The MC should inform the entertainers that he or she will ask them to come back for a bow and take their applause at the end of their performance.

Music

Music is a great aid to an MC. Besides being able to bridge the gap between time segments, it speaks an emotional language by creating ambience.

If the timing has been upset because the speeches run too long or the meal was served slowly, the music can be easily edited, acting as a kind of buffer.

The MC and DJ work closely together as a team throughout the entire event. For instance, at the entrance of the bridal party – when the MC is creating the party atmosphere – the DJ must effortlessly adjust the volume of up-vibe music to match the MC's introductions. Or when the MC calls up each speaker during the speeches, a good DJ will play a short burst of music (called a 'sting') that corresponds to the personality of each speaker and can cover any silence if the applause dies.

Unfortunately, the quality of service from some disc jockey companies has decreased over the past couple of years. While every other part of the wedding industry has lifted its game, the companies supplying music for functions have been conducting a private price war, under-cutting each other so vigorously that there is very little profit left. Consequently, staff training has been practically eliminated in an effort to cut costs. Important aspects such as how to encourage an audience to dance, how to read their moods, and microphone technique have gone by the wayside. This means that everyone suffers, including the bride and groom.

After paying for maintenance on their equipment, new CDs, and minimal wages, the only money left from their ridiculously low fee is used to give their new staff a quick lesson on how to set up the equipment. Considering the total establishment cost, the proper charge should be about the equivalent or more than an MC's fee. See 'Fees for weddings' on page 19.

The DJ as MC?

It is rare treat to find a DJ who is confident enough to use the microphone to inspire and motivate their audience. It would be even more unusual to find someone that can perform as both MC and DJ at the same time, with equal skill and equal success. Even though there are some operators who profess to do both, something must suffer and it is usually the MC role. For this arrangement to succeed, you would need an extremely competent, experienced and skilful <u>MC</u> who can also play some music – not the other way around. This person would also need a remote controller in order to play songs while they are away from the console. However, there really is no substitute for hiring someone for each job.

Lighting

Coloured lights are supplied by the music company and like DJs, they come in many different qualities. There is a huge difference in the effect between a lighting 'tree' and the usual bank of four spotlights that are placed in front of the speakers at the dancers' feet. For an MC, the mood created by music and lights is an integral part of the reception's success.

Song suggestions:

Some brides and grooms are very passionate about their music while others are happy to hear anything. The following is a guide only and might help the latter to decide.

For entry into the reception

The entry song should be up-tempo to help engender a feeling of celebration that is built into the MC's OPENING SPEECH. Ballads would get the reception off to a very slow start indeed and should be saved until the cake cutting and bridal waltz.

- Love theme from 'St Elmo's Fire' by David Foster
- 'Finally' by CeCe Peniston (From the CD Priscilla, Queen of the Desert)
- 'Celebration' by Dragon or Kool & the Gang
- 'Right On Time' by Black Box
- 'Absolutely Everybody' by Vanessa Amorosi

Cutting the Cake

The bride and groom will probably not hear much of this song because it is an important time for the photographer to take over and give them instructions on how to hold the knife and tilt their heads together. At the same time, the MC will be asking the audience to make a wish for the bride and groom (refer to RECEPTION PROCEDURE for more), and some of their friends will have come down close with their cameras. All these light-globes, instructions and good wishes tend to block out any sacred moments reserved for the special song. A classical instrumental song is good but if this proves difficult then try

- 'Tonight I Celebrate My Love' by Peabo Bryson and Roberta Flack
- 'Endless Love' by Lionel Richie and Diana Ross
- 'Kiss For A Rose' by Seal

Then it will be time for the . . .

Bridal Waltz

- 'Falling in Love with You' by Elvis Presley
- 'For the First Time' by Kenny Loggins
- 'Colour of my Love' by Celine Dion
- 'Hero' by Enrique

Conga Line

- 'Viva Las Vegas' by Elvis Presley
- 'La Bamba' by Ritchie Valens

Last song before the Bouquet

A wonderful Italian tradition is for the father to dance the last song with his daughter, the bride. 'Lauretta Mia' is a popular choice. It is the European version of 'Butterfly Kisses' – which is what a DJ would usually play on this occasion.

Circle

- 'I'm On My Way' by The Proclaimers
- '500 Miles' The Proclaimers
- 'Happy Together' by The Turtles
- 'Goin' Outa My Head (over you)' by various artists
- 'Can't Take My Eyes Off You' by Boystown Gang
- 'Sweet Caroline' by Neil Diamond
- 'I've Had The Time Of My Life' by Bill Medly & Jennifer Warnes
- 'All My Friends Are Getting Married' by Skyhooks
- 'Love and Marriage' by Frank Sinatra
- 'That's What Friends Are For' by Dionne Warwick
- 'That's Amore' by Dean Martin
- 'Oh What A Night' The Four Seasons
- '(Thank God) I'm A Country Boy' by John Denver

- 'Zorba' from the movie 'Zorba The Greek'
- 'Auld Lang Syne' A very traditional ending where all the guests in the circle cross arms and join hands with the person next to them. They can either dance to the left and right or move into and back from the circle's centre.

Guard of Honour

- 'Hit The Road Jack' by Ray Charles
- 'We Go Together' from the 'GREASE' soundtrack

Introducing speakers

Because of the special sentimental and emotional nature of weddings, many of the practices that might be considered normal in commercial public speaking are suspended at a reception. So a wedding MC who comes from a traditional public speaking background must know how to alter the rule and deliver it to suit the nuptial celebration.

A well-known formula for introducing a speaker at a business function is:

Why this speaker?
Why this subject?
Why this audience?
Why now?

It is clear that three out of the four questions have already been answered at a wedding, so the only aspect an MC needs to clarify is question number one: 'Why this speaker?' Even so, most of the guests will already know the reason why, so it is critical the MC does not spend any more time than is necessary setting it up e.g. between fifteen seconds to one minute is enough; the shorter, the better. To take question number one a bit further, here are four points a wedding MC would be wise to learn for introductions. These are:

The function the next speaker will perform, i.e. a toast or response
Their relationship to the bride and groom
Where they live (especially if they have travelled a long way)
Their name (pronounced correctly)

'Cut to the chase' when introducing one of the bride and groom's friends who has been asked to speak. For example, it is not necessary to mention the educational qualifications, type of job or accomplishments of anyone during the reception – it is not that type of event; you might even upstage the guests of honour if the introduction is too flowery.

John Haslem says: 'the master of ceremonies' job is to start the speeches on the right note and then ensure the smooth flow from one speaker to another. His speeches should be very short and he should not try to take over from the main speakers, nor should he try and dominate proceedings.'

In simple terms, an MC must make the guests aware of the <u>importance of each aspect of the entire event</u>; including the relevance of this particular person at this particular time. For instance, when introducing the parents, it is a good idea to mention how long they have been married as a statement of example to the bride and groom and credibility in the eyes of the audience.

When changing between the two fathers speaking, an MC could say *'Thank you, John, for those sincere words about our groom. We know Adam has been brought up in an atmosphere of love and support, but I once heard the father of a bride say: "It is not every day I give away a daughter, but there have been times when I've wanted to!" I am sure that is definitely not the case here, but let's find out. Would you please make welcome to the microphone, the father of the bride, Mr Bob Burrens.'*

An audience will expect the MC always to be enthusiastic. Accordingly, an MC can never be critical or negative about any part of the wedding reception, especially the speakers. As the INTRODUCTION TO SPEECH TIME says, many of the people an MC will introduce might never have spoken in public before – so the potential for embarrassment is always there.

Toasts

The toast to the bride and groom by the MC

This is the most significant toast of all, and that is why it is first on the ORDER OF SPEECHES (on page 45).

In order to set a good tone for the speeches to follow, the MC should encourage the bride and groom to choose a mature person who is familiar to both of them and is comfortable at public speaking. However, this can some-times be a 'tall order' and there is a chance that this request cannot be filled. So, as with many of the speaking roles during the wedding reception, the MC can offer to step in and give the toast themself. I have done this many times and, as you will see from the speech set out below, use my own marriage as an example.

The person giving the toast should look and gesture with an open arm towards the person being honoured.

An example (using my own marriage):

Julie and Sam have given me the honour of starting off their speeches by asking me to propose the traditional toast to the bride and groom.

Even though there are many people in this room more qualified than me to speak on the subject of matrimony, my own personal milestone was reached recently when my wife and I celebrated fourteen years of marriage – the symbol of Ivory.

All I can say is that my decision to get married was the single best decision of my life – I only wish all of my decisions had been equally successful!

And in fourteen years time, I am positive that both Julie and Sam will say the same thing about their decision to marry today.

Ladies and gentlemen, would you please all stand and raise a glass in celebration of this great match we have witnessed today, and wish them a long and happy life together . . . to Julie and Sam (the guests repeat 'Julie and Sam', take a sip and sit back down).

Toast to the parents of the bride and/or groom by the MC

Like the first-speaker role, a request for speakers to toast the bride and groom's parents will often lead to a dead-end. In this situation, the couple will be extremely grateful if the MC can offer to solve the dilemma by undertaking this combined task.

Here are two examples of how it could be done:

(When the bride and groom have been raised in an atmosphere of love, respect and trust, the MC could safely use the next toast as an emotionally rich tribute to the important team of mothers and fathers.)

Version 1

Like Julie and Sam, I was fortunate to grow up in a household surrounded by love from parents who really enjoyed their marriage.

This example of consistent friendship shown by their parents is a great basis for Julie and Sam to judge their own success as husband and wife.

With that in mind, let us all stand and congratulate Julie's parents, Enid and Ken, and Sam's parents, Dorothy and Joe, for the dedicated love and support they have shown our bride and groom . . . to Enid, Ken, Dorothy and Joe. (The guests repeat 'Enid, Ken, Dorothy and Joe', take a sip and sit back down.)

If the parents are separated or divorced, it is the job of the MC to help the bride and groom design a graceful solution to this sometimes tricky situation. The end result must be that everyone feels as though they have been suitably honoured. It is better to be up-front and ask the bride and groom how their mother and father get on – are they on pleasant speaking terms, or is there still a lot of resentment and hurt involved? Best to know in advance.

**The best thing a father can do for his children
is love their mother.**

Version 2

We all know it's a big day for Julie and Sam – but it is also a big day for the parents of the bride and groom.

Right from the moment they are born, parents wonder who their children will marry. I know, I have two little girls myself – one aged 8 and the other one is 11 – and my wife and I have already started planning their weddings!

No, seriously though, your child's wedding day is an incredibly important moment in the life of any parent. So to acknowledge that, I ask you all to stand now and raise a glass in recognition of the great job done by the parents of the bride and groom, Enid and Ken and Dorothy and Joe. (The guests repeat 'Enid, Ken, Dorothy and Joe', take a sip and sit back down.)

If a toast has been raised, then the person or group being toasted must respond – it is courtesy to do so. For instance, the best man will respond on behalf of the whole bridal party because the groom (on behalf of his wife) has raised a toast in honour of them. He will start by thanking the person who has proposed the toast.

How to write a great speech

For many guests, the speeches at a wedding reception will be the most enjoyable part of the whole occasion. It does not matter how well the speeches go, there is always a great surge in energy and a heightened atmosphere after the speakers have revealed their deepest feelings, words of advice, humorous stories and heartfelt messages of love. Allowing yourself to be vunerable to these feelings is the key to success at the podium.

Wedding speeches are a very humbling and levelling experience for most speakers. They are different from any other speaking occasion because they pinpoint a moment in time. The subject is emotional and the words are meant to enchant – two aspects that make them a recipe for great apprehension. Even with experience, people will say the strangest things when they get up to speak in front of an audience gathered to celebrate love. This pressure can magically make time and space leap into another dimension. However, the risk can be minimised if the MC encourages some prior preparation.

A child spells love as T.I.M.E.

One method to keep people's attention and entertain them at the same time is to break up the speaker's series of sincere thoughts with funny quips, quotes or anecdotes. This style works well because it gets a heartfelt message across while making people laugh at the same time. The order becomes serious / funny / serious / funny and so on. For example, the juxtaposition can be in one phrase: *'Thank you all for coming together and helping us celebrate this great day in our lives – I particularly want to make mention of those people who knew I was going to be making a speech, but turned up anyway!'* (Adapted from 'Sydney Wedding' magazine.)

Five easy rules for preparing a wedding speech

These rules (which are similar in approach to how an actor might go about preparing for a role) are a simple guide to making the speech appear personal, heartfelt and sincere.

1 A few weeks before the reception 'brainstorm' and write down a few topics, subjects or stories that you want to cover.
2 With this list in front of you, stand in a room by yourself and imagine you are at the reception, with the microphone in your hand (you could even just use a pen if you like). Start talking, and see what happens. A good start is: *'Thank you. It is a great feeling for me to be here giving this speech because . . .'*
3 After you have done this a few times, a pattern should develop. Write down the pattern, and work with it to establish a beginning, middle and an end. The opening sets the tone; the middle is the substance, while the conclusion ties everything together.
4 Stick with the pattern as an outline. Edit it into key words, topic headings or phrases that you can easily recall. Type these into a word processor and then print them out onto an A4 piece of paper (not palm-size cards) to guide you.
5 Practise . . . rehearse . . . and practise – until it sounds spontaneous!

A few things to remember

- Keep the information personal.
- Stay sober and avoid the temptation of a few drinks to 'steady the nerves'.
- Make 2 copies of your speech and give a spare copy to a guest just in case you leave it somewhere else.
- Take a moment before the speeches start to prepare and collect your thoughts away from the noise of the reception – possibly in the foyer or restroom.
- Be humble (as opposed to brash) and avoid using the opportunity to take a cheap shot at a guest.
- Flattery works best.
- Be careful of humour – no dirty stories (which are different to 'awkward moments').
- Only speak on subjects you know and in a style you are comfortable with.

Share this information among all those who intend to speak. It will be to everyone's benefit.

The groom

Part of an MC's responsibility is to help prepare the groom for his speech. Here again, groundwork is the key to a happy time with the microphone. The longer the lead time, the better the result. Magically, the brain will help a nervous groom during those critical moments in front of his guests, provided he has had enough time to plan. Encourage him to start preparing his speech at least two weeks prior to the big day. Let him know that as an experienced speaker you would never dream of speaking without notes ('off the cuff'), so neither should he.

When the groom is standing before his assembled guests, they do not expect him to be a slick professional public speaker. This information often comes as a great relief. They do, however, expect him to have done some work towards preparing what he will say on his wedding day.

A groom who gets up and starts his speech off by announcing: *'I don't know what I'm going to say, I haven't prepared anything . . .'* can hardly expect his guests to listen to any words that follow. After all, they have made an effort to get dressed up and maybe even bought a new outfit for the occasion; they have also paid out money for babysitters, bought gifts and spent a whole day with the couple. The least a groom can do is acknowledge this kindness by writing out some sincere words of appreciation beforehand.

The groom should be encouraged by the MC to incorporate the story of his courtship of the bride into his speech. It is entirely appropriate, and will always sound genuine coming from the direct source. There is usually at least one good tale attached to their romance that will often reveal a lot about the personalities of the couple concerned,

If there is a lack of speech material to be gained from the courtship, the MC can encourage the groom to look at the reasons why he has decided now, at this time in his life, to change from being single. It then becomes a powerful rite-of-passage speech, and can also incorporate the couple's plans for their future together.

Advise the groom that it is OK to mention deceased loved ones – but only if you plan it. Crying is completely appropriate at a wedding, but unscripted tears can destroy even the most seasoned of speakers.

Last, the groom would be well advised to avoid his speech becoming a 'Thank-fest'. It is tempting to show your approval by heaping praise on anyone who has had anything to do with the preparations for the wedding. However, unless the speaker says exactly what those people did to deserve the praise, it often sounds like a group of close friends patting each other on the back, and this can alienate the rest of the group and make them start to feel 'left out'.

Also, the groom sincerely saying 'Thank you' to a long list of people seldom sounds interesting and is usually boring for an audience. It should be left to a private moment alone with the person or a personal card afterwards. This is especially true for the service providers (such as the caterer) who are getting paid for their job and do not need to be thanked publicly.

This advice can come as tragic news to a groom who had planned a speech based solely on 'thanks'. In this case, the MC could recommend replacing the salutations with stories. Audiences love stories; they are personal, usually have a beginning, middle and an end and are easy to tell (and remember).

All this needs to be pointed out to the groom during the MC's interview with him.

The bride

It is becoming popular for the bride to accompany her new husband and share the microphone duties. This should be encouraged by the MC, but not pushed;

the bride has already had enough to do just to get the occasion this far, without worrying about the added pressure of public speaking.

If the bride chooses not to speak but wants to be involved in the speeches, a good alternative is for her to stand next to her husband while he is speaking. This is a very powerful symbol to the guests and looks brilliant in the photos, especially if they are speaking from the bridal table. Also, it saves the groom speaking down to his wife when he refers to her during his speech.

If it has not already been done, the bride could show her admiration of the guests who have travelled a long distance e.g. from overseas or interstate. She could lead the congratulations or applause for the sacrifice of time and the financial commitment the visitors have made to attend.

The fathers

The fathers of the bride and groom have usually lived enough of life to deliver a reasonable tribute to their children. They are proud of their child's achievements, happy with their choice of spouse, and glad to welcome the other half into the family (*'. . . I am not losing a daughter but gaining a son'*). You can probably rest assured the fathers will not embarrass themselves or the couple.

The best man

However, the same cannot be said for the best man. For some unknown reason, the best man often feels it is his duty to be hilarious, clever, heartfelt and entertaining – all in one speech at the same time. Most professional public speakers would be happy if they could even get near this accomplishment, yet many a best man will feel it's his obligation. Any dud speeches that I have witnessed at a wedding reception has usually been by the best man <u>trying too hard</u>.

These comments should not discourage the best man, but only serve as a warning. In fact, in the majority of cases, where the best man has prepared properly, his speech is an absolute highlight of the night.

Because he sits somewhere in-between the action of the protagonists, the best man starts his speech from a difficult point-of-view. It is a mark of his creativeness and ingenuity and a powerful symbol of a great male-to-male relationship if the best man can abstain from dirty jokes and just be comfortable referring to his friendship instead.

Past sexual relationships on the part of either the groom or the bride are totally inappropriate to mention. This topic should be left in the past and never referred to during any part of the reception; let the bride and groom get their marriage off to a clean start, so to speak (as referred to in 'The Keys'). Obviously, this opinion also applies to the subject of tacky mother-in-law jokes.

I publish a document called WONDERFUL WEDDING SAMPLE SPEECHES that is given to the bride and groom as part of my service to them. It has been written using actual examples from the hundreds of good and bad

The best arrangement is a set fee, with no discounts.

speeches that I have heard. This extremely helpful booklet can also be ordered separately as an email attachment from the back of this book.

Working with wedding coordinators

Unless they are <u>both</u> prepared to take on the stress, it is a lot to expect a couple to stick to a budget, follow a plan and carry out a theme (without some experience in special events). Therefore, the wedding industry has seen the rise in popularity of professional service people who 'do the lot' and organise the entire wedding process from engagement to honeymoon.

This follows a trend worldwide for expert arrangers who minimise mistakes. Many brides and grooms have busy working lives and realise the value in saved time by employing an expert coordinator.

MC's should welcome these specialist planners who, like MCs, also love to be super-organised. However, there can only be one chief, and this responsibility goes to the coordinator. They should have clear directions for the MC to follow including:

- details about the style of reception
- how they imagine the MC's presentation to fit in with this style
- what they would like the MC to wear
- the sequence and timing of the event (the run sheet)
- information on the entertainers

A 'director' or stage manager at the reception who arranges everything to a certain theme, can only add considerable value to an industry that prides itself on going that extra mile.

Fees for weddings

Some MCs are still working under the antiquated system of hourly rates. This is fine if you are being directly employed by a venue, but totally inappropriate for the normal situation where the couple employ you independently. On an hourly rate, you might not know your final wage until the time the happy couple leave the venue. This is unpredictable for them and a nuisance for you, especially if you have to chase up outstanding monies after the honeymoon.

Be certain to point out to a prospective couple that your fee includes an interview together beforehand, at either the venue or your office, help with the speeches and selection of music, and your attendance at their reception – before they arrive and until after they leave.

Unless the bride and groom are familiar with how an MC can ensure the success of their reception, it sometimes takes time for them to decide to outlay a deposit to secure your services on their special date. Point out to them that the booking for the date of their wedding is unconfirmed until a deposit is taken by you.

Once the deposit is paid (credit card facilities are very convenient for this purpose) it is best to make the bride and groom aware that full payment is appreciated before the date of the reception, usually when you meet for the interview. This saves you remembering to interrupt the happy couple during their function, when money should be the last thing on their minds. It is then another aspect of the reception that is out of the way, which means less to worry about and more time spent on making sure the bride and groom are being looked after.

Q: What personal qualities do you need to be a good lover?
A: One of you should be able to write a cheque.
Because even if you have tons of love, there is still
going to be a lot of bills.

AVA, AGE 8

If an MC becomes a permanent fixture at a certain venue, he or she can afford to drop the rate slightly if there is no pre-function work to be done.

And finally, contact the bride and groom after their honeymoon to check if they were happy with the service you offered. If there are no complaints, ask them to write a short letter about how they felt you helped the success of their wedding reception. This can then be used as a testimonial to promote your services to other prospective clients.

Using an unskilled friend

Someone without experience (or instruction and guidance from a book like this) might find it very difficult to be an effective MC. I always warn against the bride and groom using an inexperienced friend to conduct the sometimes stressful and exacting reception – especially since there is only *one* chance to get it right. They may as well let their mate just enjoy the event like the rest of their guests.

The only occasion where an unskilled person could take the reins as an MC is where the bride and groom have consciously decided to have a low-key, quiet reception like a cocktail party.

After I surveyed many brides and grooms, the five main reasons they gave for having a friend or relative as their MC were:

- They wanted to save *money*.
- They did not know *how* to hire a professional MC.
- The function manager did not *know* of any professional MCs.
- The MC *volunteered* because he wanted the experience.
- They were worried that an 'outside' MC might not understand their family *traditions* or speak their language.

Let's take all of these legitimate concerns one by one.

First, the cost of an MC pales into insignificance once the bride and groom realise how much an MC does to make their wedding reception a success. If the couple have professionals to handle every other part of their wedding, why should they stop at the MC? Relative to what the other professionals charge, an MC's fee is very reasonable, especially when you break it down into an hourly rate.

The MC connects the couple with their guests via the clever use of their personality – while the other professionals do it via their food (the caterers), their music (DJ or band), their film (video and photographers), decoration (chair-covers) and flowers (florist). They are all equally important so why risk using an amateur in one area?

The second and third points involve function and banquet managers. Staff from the catering department of a hotel are doing themselves (and their client) a great favour by recommending the use of a professional MC at each function held at their premises. The venue can look at this additional service and advice to their client as **adding value**. The manager can give the MC's name and contact details to the client when they are discussing catering arrangements for the function.

When a function manager suggests the client use a professional MC, they are intelligently protecting their own reputation, and guaranteeing a good result for all concerned. This reflects well on everyone and leaves a good impression in the minds of the guests. (Refer to Foreword I and II.)

Hospitality personnel at quality hotels and venues are selected with the utmost precision, and the same care is usually exercised when allowing an MC to join that team, even if it is only for one night. Therefore, from their point of view, it is wise to find a reliable MC whose style and professionalism matches that of the venue.

The great reputation of some hotels takes years to establish, but it can easily be destroyed overnight by one unsuccessful function. A professional MC can serve as a 'human insurance policy' that protects both reputations and preparations. If an inexperienced MC is permitted to take the reins at a function in a reputable venue, the function manager is risking the renown of the establishment, the satisfaction of the client and ultimately his or her own job security.

Most guests assume the MC is attached to the venue – whether they are or not – so it makes a lot of sense to use their service. For more information on how to book top quality MCs, visit www.weddingmc.com.au

The fourth point is tricky for a bride and groom. Some couples worry about offending their friend by saying 'No' to the kind offer to MC their wedding reception. The fun aspect of having someone who is familiar as their MC also tempts them – plus they could save some cash. These are all legitimate reasons, but the choice of an MC is a serious decision and should not be taken too lightly.

The bride and groom who decide to use an inexperienced friend to MC their important wedding must seriously think about whether they are doing the correct thing by themselves, their guests and their friend. If he or she has not had any training in the skills outlined in this book, then the friend should go and practise at some *other* function – not the wedding of this bride and groom! If the wedding is many months away, then there is possibly time to join a group like 'Toastmasters' and enrol in their excellent 'Speech Craft' course.

It makes sense for the function manager
to recommend that the client use a professional MC.

Otherwise, the bride and groom could buy this book as a pre-reception 'Thank You' gift to the intending master of ceremonies. Apart from that, the other way to gain skills is to watch and observe experienced MCs at their work. I sometimes invite MCs who want guidance to watch and scrutinise me as they learn.

One way a bride and groom can tactfully discourage an untried friend who has innocently offered to MC for free is to point out the huge responsibilities involved in the job. These include not drinking, limited time to dance and socialise, plus the considerable time needed to prepare.

Lastly, as far as families and their different traditions go (point number five), it is the duty of any professional – including the MC – to be aware of and know how to achieve the unique wishes of the couple. An MC must be sensitive to different cultures and weave them effortlessly into their presentation and the theme of the night. The guests will welcome any special tradition that is introduced, because it helps to separate this wedding reception from the last one they attended, or any other.

The future for wedding MCs

Books like this will help MCs to realise how they can educate the public to the advantages of using our essential service; so we become one of the first decisions that a bride and groom make after they have selected a venue.

The Australian Wedding Professionals (AWP) are a group of industry experts who hold wedding information evenings that are fun, educational and entertaining. They have identified a need to provide unbiased material to brides and grooms that cover most aspects of planning a wedding and a way of evaluating possible services – something the original bridal fairs were meant to do.

In their handbook, which is distributed at these information evenings, the AWP identify five key areas in which a professional MC has distinct advantages:

1 A professional will be accustomed to the responsibilities of the other professionals (DJ, photographer, video-person, functions manager) working at the reception. There is an immediate understanding and rapport that helps in the execution of each job.
2 The MC's experience allows them to anticipate and deal directly with any problems that arise. This can be done with ease, without disrupting the flow of the evening or disturbing the guests.
3 A professional MC is familiar with the timing of events; skilled to coordinate each step and make any necessary adjustments on the go.
4 Great MCs have the talent to bring every phase of the reception together to create an appropriate environment – taking into account the personalities of the bride and groom.
5 Using the abilities mentioned above, the MC provides an added touch of class by making the reception unique and creating a feeling that the guests are at a very special event.

The handbook also lists the qualities that a couple should look for when choosing their MC:

Experience
There is no MC school so proficiency is learnt by on-the-job experience.

Adaptability
An MC should be flexible and adjust to different cultural traditions.

An attitude of fun
Someone who inspires excitement and celebration in the hearts of the guests.

Humility
The bride and groom remain the centre of attention for the entire reception.

Use this list to teach the public about your valuable service. You may like to add that an excellent MC will leave the bride and groom more time to talk with their guests so they do not have to worry about 'what happens next?'

Q: How can you make love last?
A: Don't forget your wife's name. That will mess up the love.

DICK, AGE 7

Some final advice for the Master of Ceremonies

- *MC etiquette* – Even though you might like to show off your cute bum to the assembled guests, it is probably better if you do not lean across the bridal table to speak to the bride and groom, but rather go around the back, bend down and whisper in their ear instead.
- Remember these are joyous times, so do not be too earnest or grave about the information or message you are giving out – be happy and remember to smile. In fact, if the MC looks as though they are having fun at this party, the audience will too. As Ron Tacchi says: 'If you're enjoying it – tell your face about it.'
- If one or more of the bridal party are involved in the speeches, the MC can introduce them with *'Now let's hear from our bridal party what it has been like to be a best friend to .... (the bride) and .... (the groom)'.*
- After an emotional speech, the MC could show their mixture of elation and exhaustion by saying: *'Gee, I feel like a cigarette – and I don't even smoke!'* or *'Can I ask for a big box of tissues to each table please?'*
- Once the speeches have finished and the lectern isn't going to be used again, move it to the side and out of the way.

- If you are leaving the room for any length of time, e.g. to eat or relax while the dancing is on, make sure you let the banquets manager know exactly where you will be – just in case they need you quickly. Take your mobile phone.

Some final advice for the bride and groom

- Reception houses like to follow tradition and place the dance floor directly in front of the bridal table. This is not always the best position since the large empty space consumes 'energy' and keeps the guests from being close and intimate. In my opinion, the dance floor is better situated away from the main area to the side.
- If possible, practise your bridal waltz in a gown resembling your wedding dress. Designers do not consider how difficult it might be to dance for an hour or two in this lovely-looking but totally impractical creation. A detachable 'train' is highly-recommended for this reason.
- Unless your watch is crucial to the look of the dress or has sentimental value, I recommend not wearing one at all. If the MC is doing their job correctly, they should be all the time-piece you will need.

Photographers: When selecting a photographer or videographer, look beyond the quality of their photos. Ask them what they will wear on the day; it is often below the standard of everyone else and can make a mockery of your other guest's careful choice of attire.

Many photographers wear those dreadful old Army jackets with lots of pockets because it suits their preferred image of what they would rather be doing e.g. a tough photo-journalist taking important, artful slides that will end up in National Geographic. The photographer will say the jackets are necessary to hold spare film, but this can be done with any coat.

Many will not say as much, but consider bridal photography to be at the end of the food chain when it comes to level of 'coolness'. If they are very <u>proud</u> to be wedding photographers, they will be also proud enough to wear the appropriate clothes e.g. a suit, to compliment your event.

It is now half time. Please enjoy your interval. The second half will be starting soon . . .

Drawing by Chris Breckwoldt

A wedding should not resemble a business function

And now for the main feature . . .

Templates

I suggest you photocopy the following templates and enlarge them to A4 size so they fit comfortably in a good quality black folder (not a clipboard). Print them on coloured paper – a different colour for each – so you can identify them at a glance. Alternatively, they are available as a Microsoft WORD email attachment that you can manipulate from www.compere.com.au

The main two forms are the WEDDING PARTY DETAILS and the RECEPTION PROCDURE. When completed, they contain all the material necessary to guide an MC through the event and make them seem like one of the family – which is what everyone wants the MC to be. These forms are the paste that sticks the whole night together.

I send these two forms to the couple and ask them to complete and return them both at least two weeks prior to their reception. After this, I can either meet personally with the couple and go through the entire reception plan or discuss the contents over the phone. The bride and groom should be able to finish this meeting with a great feeling of relief knowing that every aspect of their reception is under control. And the MC should leave knowing that he or she has all the necessary details to ensure that the event will run smoothly.

It needs to be stressed that preparation before the event is the best way to prevent any surprises. Part of this homework is to ask the bride and groom all the necessary questions before the reception, so the MC is not interrupting them while they are trying to enjoy their own party.

Explanation of the MC's CHECKLIST

If you are consistently working at weddings, you may find it easier to develop a 'uniform'. To streamline the whole process of preparation, invest some time thinking about what looks best as your MC attire, then purchase it and use it only for wedding work.

I found my first suit at a formal hire sale. I bought a matching bow tie and handkerchief, patent leather shoes and a formal 'studded' shirt all at the same time, and this became my standardised clothes for every wedding.

For men, black bow ties are more appropriate at a wedding than anywhere else – perhaps because so many men wear normal ties during the working week. Talking of which, a wedding should not resemble a business function in any way – except for the efficiency of those working. In a similar vein, the MC should not start by welcoming 'Distinguished guests' or mention the 'housekeeping' or be referred to by others as 'Mr Chairman'.

To ensure I work with excellent (and familiar) equipment, I have purchased my own small, unobtrusive personal public address (PA) system that I can easily carrry in the boot of my car. I use it at about 95% of weddings because it allows me the freedom of working with a cordless microphone.

The MC'S CHECKLIST

Preparation at home

Shirts ironed / shoes polished / suit dry cleaned

Briefcase: Good quality blue ink pens, black folder
This entire book with all the sections completed
Copies for each speaker of the ORDER OF SPEECHES
Clothes brush / fresh breath mints / toothbrush & paste
Business cards + display holder / name badge
Voice warm-up tape / mobile phone / wrist-watch
Sound system / personal PA (optional)
10 × old keys for 'The Keys' game
Street directory

Your (early) arrival at the venue

Function Manager: Check serving times / menu or buffet?
Professionals' meals?
Smoking allowed?
Location of rest rooms
Location of light dimmer
Location of gift table
How will guests know where they are sitting?

Check house microphone level & lectern placement

Disc Jockey: synchronise music selections

Arrival of bridal party

Meet and make them feel welcome. Introduce yourself (usually in the ante-room). Check if drinks and appetisers are needed.

Organise the order of entry into the reception.

Entrance *lights up*

Photographer and Video-person ready to film?

Use WEDDING PARTY DETAILS and MC'S OPENING SPEECH

Grace (if required)

'Dear Lord, please bless this gathering here tonight and the food we are about to partake; for what we are about to receive, may we be truly thankful. Be present at our table on this very special occasion, but most of all, let us pray for the bride and groom; may they have a long and happy life together. Amen'

(*If Catholic*) In the name of the Father, Son and the Holy Spirit. Amen.

Dinner *lower lights*
Distribute copies of the ORDER OF SPEECHES and one for yourself
Edit telegrams
Enquire whether any cards from bouquets need to be read out
Set up 'The Keys' (if appropriate)

Speeches *lights up*
Use   INTRODUCTION TO SPEECH TIME
        RECEPTION PROCEDURE
        AUDIENCE GAMES
        INTERVIEW
Check Photographer ready?
        Videographer ready?
        DJ ready with 'stings'? (see Music)
        Lights have been brightened?
        Special gifts ready to be presented? e.g. flowers
        Extra glasses of champagne next to the lectern
Refer to 'Explanation of the RECEPTION PROCEDURE' for a complete summary of what is expected from here on till the end of the event.

Cake cutting

Bridal waltz *lower lights*

Dancing Take a rest and have your meal now – you deserve it!

In the last ¾ hour
Announce last songs
Remind the bride and groom of what is about to happen
Collect the bouquet (sometimes kept in the refrigerator)
Check for arrival of get-away car
Secure the couple's luggage in the boot of the get-away car

Bouquet *lights up*

Garter

Circle

Guard of honour

'Farewell' The MC says goodnight

Explanation of the WEDDING PARTY DETAILS

The focus here is on attention to detail.

Proper <u>pronunciation</u> of names is essential if you are to have any credibility in the eyes of the assembled audience – getting the names wrong will immediately label you as an outsider. There is absolutely no excuse for incorrectly articulating the names of those honoured members of the bridal party when you introduce them.

Once the list is returned at the interview, note any difficult or unusual names. Verify the pronunciation with the bride or groom, write them out phonetically and practise saying them aloud. Ring the bride and groom before the wedding if you need to confirm your pronunciation. At the very least, say them with confidence so as to give the impression that they were correct!

If some of the bridal party are related to the bride and groom, it is a good idea to write next to their names the nature of the relationship. You can then use this handy information (and make yourself seem like one of the family) when you introduce them. For example: *'Put your hands together as we welcome our first bridesmaid and groomsman couple, the bride's sister Julie Smith, accompanied by the groom's younger brother Darren Jones.'*

The individual members of a bridal party can be a great help to an MC. If they take their role seriously (instead of getting inebriated), there are jobs you can delegate to the right people. They will feel appreciated, and enjoy the task of assisting the success of the event.

When introducing the parents, you might like to mention how long they have been married as a great example for the bride and groom to emulate.

It does not happen often, but a bride may want to keep her maiden name, so this question needs to be asked, and the decision recorded in the space provided.

The 'Extras' section at the end is for any other information that might be useful but not covered. For example, the MC might like to mention the disposable cameras on the table or ask everyone to complete the guest book as it gets passed from table to table.

The WEDDING PARTY DETAILS are also useful to keep on file in case you wish to send the bride and groom a one-year anniversary card.

WEDDING PARTY DETAILS

Date of Wedding_____   # of Guests_____
Venue _____   Phone No _____
Address _____
Function Room_____   Function Manager _____
Time: from _____   to _____

The Names of Everyone Involved

Bride_____   Groom _____
H-Phone _____   H-Phone_____
W-Phone_____   W-Phone _____

In order of introduction (refer to MC'S OPENING SPEECH)

Parents

Bride's Mother _____   Groom's Mother _____
Bride's Father_____   Groom's Father _____

Bridal Party

Flower girl(s) _____   Page boy(s) _____
Bridesmaid _____   Groomsman _____
Bridesmaid _____   Groomsman _____
Bridesmaid _____   Groomsman _____
Matron of Honour_____   Best Man _____

Bride and Groom

Announced as Mr and Mrs _____

Professionals

Photographer _____
Video Cameraman _____
Disc Jockey _____
Extras e.g. Dancers, Limo Drivers, etc. _____

Explanation of the RECEPTION PROCEDURE

The traditional format of a wedding reception is a great asset to the MC. Starting with the path laid down in the run sheet known as the RECEPTION PROCEDURE, the MC must allow the bride and groom to feel that the format is <u>flexible</u> and serves only as a guide that they can alter if they wish to personalise the structure of their occasion. This empowers the couple to feel that the reception represents their combined needs, and also gives them a sense of originality.

Be careful not to stray too far from the traditional blueprint that has worked for generations. There are many obligations at any kind of wedding reception, and each of these must be given its full recognition. On the other hand, it is the bride and groom's function and the MC can only advise them to a certain extent.

The MC should arrive at the reception venue at least half an hour before the scheduled time for guests' cocktails. Refer to the MC's CHECKLIST for details of who to speak to first and what areas should be covered in this important initial half hour before any of the visitors appear.

One point an MC must remember is to give the other professionals plenty of notice when something is about to occur. It fact, it is a good idea to run through the entire RECEPTION PROCEDURE with them at the beginning of the event. They hate to be surprised!

You might find the bridal party either outside still having photographs taken or perhaps relaxing in the ante-room / bridal suite supplied for them by the venue. Encourage the bride and groom to build this break-time into their schedule, especially if the ceremony was many hours before. It is a time to freshen up and compose themselves for the next stage of the wedding. However, the photographer will often use this opportunity to keep clicking – after all, that is their job – and once the bride and groom have entered the reception there is little chance to capture any more of the evocative, romantic shots that are the wedding photographer's stock-in-trade.

If the bridal party has not turned up from the photographic session, seek out the bride's and groom's parents; you have their names on the WEDDING PARTY DETAILS form, so why not make them feel welcome? Let them know when (or if) you will be introducing them, and where. You can also start to get a feel for what type of people you will be dealing with over the course of the evening.

Check the sequence of place names at the bridal table before you start to organise the order of entry. Is it all ladies on one side and men on the other?

When the bridal party are together as a group, introduce yourself confidently to them. Once they are gathered in the ante-room or are ready to enter the reception (with or without the parents), explain how the introduction of each couple will occur and confirm the correct pronunciation of all their names. It is also at this point that the bride and groom should hand over complete control and entrust the MC to be their spokesperson and smoothly make their wishes come to life.

RECEPTION PROCEDURE

Guests arrive for cocktails .... PM

Bridal Party entry-pairing (right or left) to copy bridal table .... PM

Bride & Groom enter (up-tempo song) ....

Grace? (to be read by) ....

Dinner Will speeches be held   (Circle)

After Entree?   After Mains?   After Dessert?

Traditional order of speeches (guide only)
(European Order is # 5,7,3,2)

1 Toast to Bride & Groom proposed by ....

2 Response & Toast to the Bridal Party by the Groom/Bride ....

3 Response on behalf of the Bridal Party by the Best
   Man/Matron Of Honour ....

4 Toast to the Bride's Parents by ....

5 Response by the Bride's Father ....

6 Toast to the Groom's Parents by ....

7 Response by the Groom's Father ....

8 Special Messages e.g. Telegrams/faxes/emails/cards read by ....

(With speeches after Mains, **Dessert** can be served here or during dancing)

Cutting of the Wedding **Cake** (suggest instrumental song) ....

Bridal **Waltz** (songs) ....

(Will the others join in during the first song or at the start of the 2nd song?)

Dancing	Yes / No	Time ....
Bouquet/Garter	Yes / No	Time ....
Farewell Circle	Yes / No	Time ....
(This should be quick – suggest sing-a-long)		
Guard of Honour/Archway	Yes / No	Time ....

Note: When working with hotel wedding supervisors, it is advisable to let them escort the bridal party down from their bridal suite in readiness to be introduced from the foyer.

Once you have moved the bridal party into the correct order of introduction outside the doors to the reception, encourage them to smile and look happy as they make their way into the room buoyed by a lively tune (see Song Suggestions). Note: This does not work using a ballad.

Traditionally, the parents of bride and groom enter first; if they are not sitting at the bridal table, then they can sit down after they have entered the room. The venue staff is usually on hand to open the doors as each couple enter and are introduced, and also to pull out the chair for each member of the bridal table as they take their positions. Ask them to stand behind their seats until the bride and groom are announced.

A smile is the lighting system for the face
and the heating system for the heart.

Because all the preparations have been made, as decided beforehand in consultation with the functions manager and the MC, the bride and groom can now confidently enter their wedding reception. They should not need to worry about *'what comes next?'* They can relax completely and enjoy the company of their family and friends, comfortable in the knowledge that the MC will look after every little thing.

Grace (optional)

If the Minister who officiated at the ceremony is not attending and the bride and groom have not nominated anyone else, then the saying of Grace naturally falls to the MC.

Depending upon the impending arrival of the first course, Grace can be said as everyone is still standing and the bridal party have finally finished taking their places at the bridal table, or just before the entree is served.

The second arrangement is preferable but it is not always practical. The disadvantage of saying Grace directly after the bridal party enters the room is the anti-climatic formality after such a high-tempo entrance. A sample religious Grace has been provided in the WEDDING MC's CHECKLIST otherwise I heard this lovely non-religious blessing:

Let us give thanks for the food we are about to receive.
Let us give thanks to the bride's parents for providing this wonderful
wedding celebration.
Let us give thanks to family and friends who came to bear witness to
the marriage.
Let us also remember those family and friends not here today but are
here with us in spirit instead.

May the bride and groom be poor in misfortune but rich in blessings.
May they be slow to make enemies but quick to make friends.
Rich or poor, quick or slow – may they know nothing but happiness from
this day forward.

Dinner

The choice of having speeches after the main meal or after dessert is sometimes determined by the venue and their catering department. Obviously the venue has a staffing agenda and everyone must do their best to work with it.

If there is a choice, the MC should discuss the advantages of each before the big day and explain to the bride and groom the consequences of each of the three, as outlined below:

Having speeches after the *main meal* is the healthier option because it offers a break between courses. However, with this arrangement the dessert runs the risk of being ignored because it is served while people are dancing. This can be avoided by having a short break while dessert is served immediately after reading the telegrams, followed by the cake cutting and the waltz. However, these breaks will reduce the all-important dancing time.

The advantage of finishing all three courses is that the evening has a flow to it; it is not broken up by different stages. The guests have a lot of time to mix with each other (and the bride and groom) before the loud music of the disco starts. Unfortunately, three courses piled on top of one another can really sap the energy of the group.

The MC and other professionals can also use this time to grab a chance to eat what is known as a 'service' meal. It is usually only a main course – advise the bride and groom that they should be charged a reduced rate for these meals. Otherwise, the MC can relax and eat later while the dancing is going on.

A complete reversal of all these arrangements is to conduct the speeches and cake cutting at the beginning of the reception, immediately following the entry of the bridal party. This is good for the speakers as they can then relax, but it provides no climatic counterpoint to the meal. If the speeches are over early in the reception, there is not much the MC can do to create a flow of events. Also, if the speeches go on for a while, there is the risk of upsetting the chef, and the hungry guests might get restless.

Once again, it needs to be stressed that the RECEPTION PROCEDURE is a traditional format, but it should be treated as flexible.

Speeches

Speeches are a wonderful tool for changing the atmosphere and making sure the room is filled with joy, laughter and maybe a few tears. Every one of these emotions is entirely appropriate but how they are handled depends upon the preparation and personality of who is speaking.

The order of the speeches shown on the template is a traditional one and can be altered to suit. The European order is for each of the fathers to speak first, followed by the best man, and then the groom to finish.

> ☑ **A TIP:** The most help an MC can be to anyone is to prepare them for what is about to happen and thereby avoid any awkwardness; in other words; to anticipate the inevitable. Guard against any embarrassment to the hosts by remembering to remind them of the simple things like visiting the restrooms before the speeches start.

Telegrams

People who were invited to the reception but were not able to attend traditionally send a telegram in place of their absence. This is an old custom, and many young people in the audience would not even be aware of what a genuine telegram looks like. However, there is a trend now for the assembled guests to take this opportunity to insert a few fictitious telegrams of a lewd nature, which are meant to embarrass the bride and / or groom in front of their families.

The MC should not encourage these telegrams (usually produced via writing pads provided on the tables); they are rarely funny, waste valuable time and lower the whole tone of the event to that of a bucks night. If it proceeds, then the MC might have to edit the offensive ones.

Candles

Before they cut the cake, the bride and groom might elect to each light a candle (from the same match). The MC could accompany this ritual with: *'The lighting of each candle signifies the light of love that shall burn for the rest of their lives together and the heat of the flame signifies the warmth in their hearts for each other. As each year passes, two candles will again be lit on the anniversary of this day, to remember this moment.'*

Alternatively, the MC can light two candles and hand one each to the bride and groom. During the next overture, the bride and groom light a third candle from the flame of their individual candles: *'These two candles signify the separate lives that the bride and groom have led up to this moment. As they join their two flames to light the single flame, so their lives are also joined.'*

Exchange of rings

When a bride and groom have different religions, they have 3 choices:

1 One of them can convert to the other religion and partake in that particular ceremony

2 They can have two different ceremonies

3 They can bypass the ceremony altogether and get married at a registry. If this is the case, a formal exchange of rings procedure can take place at the reception. An appropriate verse from the MC might go something like: *'The exchange of rings between the bride and groom is a very traditional part of any wedding and has been the custom for centuries. Each ring symbolises eternal love, the never-ending circle of trust and the bonds that cannot be broken between the wearers of the rings. Let's now congratulate the Lord and Lady of the Rings'*. (Apologies to JRR Tolkien.)

Cutting of the cake

The cutting of the cake is one of the first duties that a husband and wife will perform together. Like the bridal waltz, it is a romantic moment for everyone. However, in some traditions, the romance is cut short by the couple spreading cake and cream all over each other's face! This practice comes from the ancient fertility symbol where the bride was showered with wheat confetti (or rice). The wheat developed into small sweet cakes during the Roman era but the throwing of food remained as an interlude of fun.

As the lower section of the INTERVIEW page has prompted you to ask, the cake will often have been donated or baked and decorated by one of the guests so it is an appropriate time to acknowledge this kind gesture. Apart from that, the cake is usually a spectacular work of art and deserves some mention for its artistic value.

If the cake is located on or near the dance-floor, you can ask the guests to stand and form a circle around the bride and groom, especially if the vision of everyone is limited by the cake's location. Invite the guests to come forward and use their cameras. The official photographer usually likes to direct the couple. Also, as the bride and groom cut their cake and make a wish, ask all the guests to *'. . . make a collective wish for the happiness of the bride and groom'*.

A distinctive touch is to ask a staff member to make another slice in the cake and remove the first piece onto a plate. The groom then feeds a spoonful to his bride, and vice-versa. This commences the eating of their ceremonial cake. It is then whisked away by the venue staff, cut up, put into little sachets, and distributed by the bridesmaids to each guest. Encourage the guests to take some home for the next day and eat it as a memory of the event.

Invite the bride and groom to wash down their cake with champagne; here another opportunity presents itself for everyone to raise a glass (or goblet) and toast as the happy couple link arms and drink from the 'loving cup'.

In a more formal setting, the MC could add that drinking from the loving cup *'. . . symbolises the intertwining of two lives, two loves and two hearts – now joined as one'*.

Bridal waltz (see also Song Suggestions)

If the guests are not already standing, the MC can ask them to form a circle around the dance floor (if this seems appropriate). After the lights have been lowered and the bride and groom are waltzing – or simply just *swaying* – the MC should prepare their parents and the bridal party to join the couple on the dance floor. Announce each pair (as organised beforehand with the bride and groom) during the first song, or at the beginning of the second song; which is usually a ballad.

Sometimes the second song is taken up with the bride sharing a dance with her father and the groom with his mother.

By the end of the song, the bridal party have usually had ample opportunity to shuffle around and change partners and it is time to invite the remaining guests to '. . . *grab their partner by the hand and share this romantic moment with the bride and groom by joining them on the dance floor'*. An MC can really help the DJ here by encouraging everyone to join in.

At this point the MC can look forward to a well-earned rest. They might personally congratulate the speakers who did well and hand over the reins to the DJ by announcing that he or she will take requests.

Throwing the bouquet

This practice is similar in origin to the wedding cake fertility symbol mentioned earlier. The unmarried young women of the Roman era were expected to scramble for the remaining grains of wheat (or rice) to ensure their own betrothals after the bride had been showered with confetti.

This has developed into the modern ritual of all the single and 'unattached' women gathering at one end of the dance floor to catch a bouquet of flowers thrown by the bride over the back of her head. Warn the bride not to toss the bunch too high and hit the roof and then count down from '3'.

The tradition says that the lucky girl who catches the bouquet will be the next to be married. This is always a lot of fun and I finish by making a request for all their phone numbers!

The Wedding Bouquet

You are at the wedding . . .
You are a total Diva . . .
The best dress, a perfect hairdo . . .
You fall in love with an invited guest . . .
You get secret looks the entire night . . .
On the dance floor, he's by your side constantly, and he dances like a god . . .
You are the couple of the evening . . .
The anticipated moment has arrived for all single women . . .
The bride is about to throw the bouquet . . .

You are first in line, in a strategic position . . .
Once there, you wait for the right moment . . .
You look at him sensually, and with your eyes you tell him . . .
If I catch the bouquet . . . <u>I Will Marry You!</u>
And then, the moment you've been waiting for . . .
The bride throws the bouquet . . .
He doesn't stop looking at you . . .
You jump like never before to catch the bouquet . . .
Your arms stretched out . . .
Your hands open . . .
And suddenly . . .

Catching the garter

All the bachelors do the same as the ladies except instead of flowers the guys jump for a silk garter that has just been removed by the groom from around the bride's leg – in time to some seductive music. The MC should set this up by asking the bride to either sit or elegantly rest her leg and foot on the seat of a chair.

The groom can also be blind-folded and hand-cuffed so he has to grab at the garter with his teeth. (I always offer to help – but I have never had any takers?). Once he has the garter, he can stand up, be spun around and given the general direction to throw in.

In the modern era of wedding ritual, the garter and bouquet can be seen as politically-incorrect and some coercion might need to be applied by the MC to persuade the reluctant would-be bride and grooms out onto the dance floor. Also, if there are not a lot of potential suitors, the MC can combine the throwing of the bouquet and garter together so it becomes a 'meeting place' of the single people in the room. Otherwise, it can be all ladies (un-attached or not) for the flowers and all men for the garter.

The MC can then match up the garter-catching man with the girl who caught the bouquet and make it a photo opportunity.

Farewell circle

The bride starts by saying goodbye to the groom's parents first, then his grooms-men, and subsequently moves around the circle, ending with her saying goodbye to her bridesmaids and, last of all, to her parents. At the same time the groom goes the opposite way, ending by saying goodbye to his groomsmen and then his parents. This order makes the parents feel very special (refer to the diagram).

The only problem is the (lack of) energy of the (sober) guests and the length of time this operation takes to unfold. Good sing-a-long songs from the DJ (see Song Suggestions) plus some encouragement to join in from the MC à la karaoke, can really help pass the time.

If this sequence does not drag on too long, the circle can become the emotional high point of the evening, especially towards the end when the bride and groom are saying farewell to their respective parents. Woe betides the MC who interrupts at this crucial spot.

Depending on the venue, streamers and confetti can be liberally strewn across the circle.

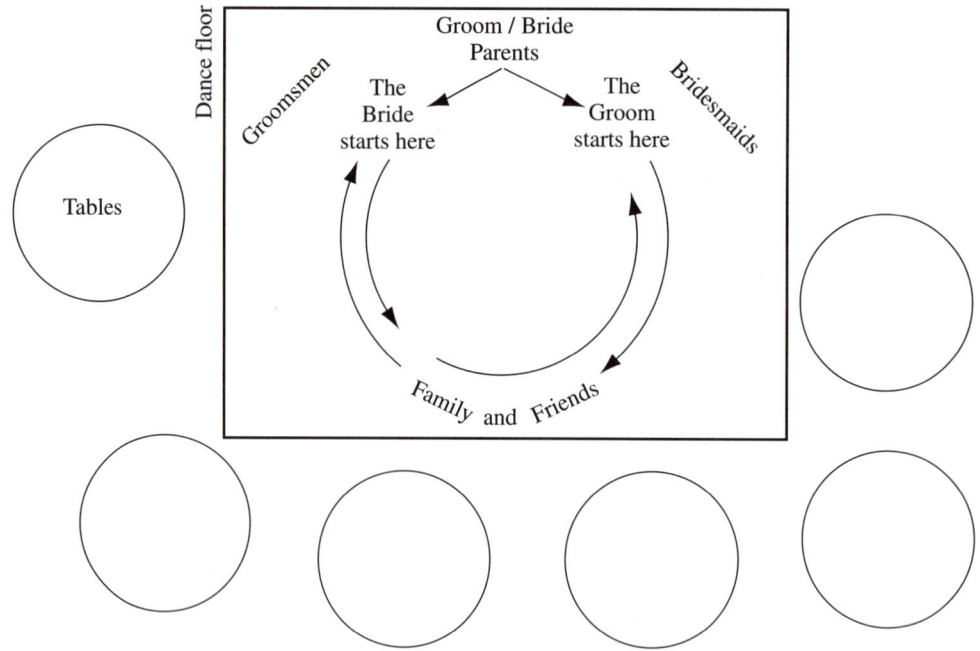

The farewell circle

Guard of honour

All the people in the circle now come together in a line and then raise their arms to form an archway that the bride and groom must run through. This is quick, fun, and a neat way to finish a big day.

If the bride and groom are worried about getting tickled too much, you can suggest that the guests form a wide passageway for the couple to make their departure. This can also substitute the traditional Circle as a preference. Otherwise, on the prompting of the MC to shout 'three cheers', the bride and groom can simply move to the exit, wave goodbye and leave the room via the door closest to where they will either hop into the 'get-away car' or catch a lift to their room.

The honeymoon

Audiences are often interested to learn the source of the expression 'honeymoon' and consequently the details of where the bride and groom are travelling away to after the reception. 'Drinking honey wine makes the first month of marriage the sweetest' is a well-known reason for its origin, however the term 'honeymoon' literally translates as the first month of marriage.

Presents

It is the MC's responsibility to organise for the gifts to be safely removed from the reception. A hotel staff member will be able to assist with a trolley and delivery to the bridal suite if the bride and groom are staying overnight. Otherwise, the parents or the members of the bridal party should see that any presents are secured on behalf of the bride and groom – who by this time have left for romantic wedding-night photographs or are driving to their overnight stay, to the cheers of the passing motorists. It could be a while before the bride and groom return from their honeymoon and have a chance to open the gifts, so it is essential that the job be left with someone who is sober, reliable and can store them safely.

The table flower arrangements are often available to be taken home. Many guests would love to do this if they could so the MC should check with the venue if this is possible and announce it at the very end.

Q: Why does love happen between two people?
A: No one is sure why it happens, but I heard
it has something to do with how you smell.
That's why perfume and deodorants are so popular.

Mae, age 9

At the end of the reception, after the bride and groom have gone, the MC must wrap the event up swiftly. A short announcement over the microphone inviting everyone back inside the venue to collect their possessions, wishing them all a safe journey home and reminding them to '. . . *not drive any faster than your guardian angel can fly'* is usually enough. If there is a nightclub close by, the MC can direct the revellers there to keep on partying.

Explanation of the MC's OPENING SPEECH

The MC's opening speech sets the tone for rest of the event. You will notice that it is written in a style that gives permission for the guests to change from the restrained and religious gathering of the marriage ceremony to the celebratory party that is now about to begin; from formal to informal.

People in social situations like to be organised and directed – so a confident invitation from the MC to have fun is a welcome sign.

The first part of the speech is an 'icebreaker', allowing the audience and the MC to quickly gauge each other. Wait for a response, and then react to what you are given back from the audience. If you feel it is not enough, then encourage everyone to respond with a bit more gusto. It will pay off handsomely when they come to cheer for the bride and groom in a few minutes time.

If the venue has supplied a cordless microphone, you have the luxury of announcing from either the lectern, the dance floor or in amongst the tables. Otherwise, the lectern is the traditional place from which the MC would normally do all the announcements, including the opening speech.

Spaces have been left to fill in the names, but if you feel confident enough, refer to the names from the completed WEDDING PARTY DETAILS attached to the other side of your folder.

Besides welcoming the guests, the MC has to create a positive atmosphere that is appropriate for the bridal party's grand entrance. The introduction of the parents, the bridal party and the bride and groom is an extremely important part of the wedding reception. This importance needs to be clear in the mind of the MC so that he or she can then transfer this enthusiasm to everyone concerned.

The MC'S OPENING SPEECH

(just before Bride & Groom enter)

Ladies & Gentlemen, it is with great pleasure that I welcome you here tonight on this lovely evening at (venue) .... to celebrate the wedding of (B&G) ....

My name is .... and I have the honour of being your MC, your Master of Ceremonies, for this wonderful event.

Earlier today, everyone attended a dignified ceremony where (B&G) .... professed their love for each other. It is now time to celebrate that love, so I hope you are all set to party and create some wonderful happy memories. Are you ready to have a great time?

With the expert staff here at the (venue) .... + our video cameraman .... our photographer .... and your DJ .... we'll do every thing possible to make this an enjoyable and memorable celebration for everyone.

But in order to create that memorable occasion, we need some vital ingredients. Most of them are here already – such as a beautiful meal waiting to be served, this decorated room filled with good friends, relations and the people that mean the most to (B&G) ....

So, the recipe is nearly set. Really the only thing missing, the most important ingredient of all is the happy couple themselves and their bridal party. So let me introduce them to you – I won't ask you to stand until the B&G come in.

With your applause please make welcome the **Parents** of the Bride/Groom ....

It is indeed an honour to be asked to be part of a bridal party, and that honour today goes to our **Bridesmaid** .... accompanied by **Groomsman** .... etc.

It's an even greater honour to be asked to be **Chief Bridesmaid/Maid of Honour & Best Man**. Please make welcome with your applause

....

Now if it wasn't for these next two people falling in love, none of us would be here right now. So let's stand and make them feel very special. With your cheers and applause (or money!) lets raise the roof and welcome the world's newest husband and wife (**Bride & Groom**) Mr and Mrs ....

GRACE? (While everyone is still standing)

This is a non-smoking venue, so if you would like to partake of a cigarette, please do so out in the foyer. The rest rooms are located ....
....
I'll leave you now in the capable hands of the staff who will shortly serve you a lovely 3-course meal. If you need to know anything at all, please ask the staff or myself. Until then, I bid you 'Bon Appetiff' and I'll be back before you can say 'I do'.

Explanation of the ORDER OF SPEECHES

As a value-added service to the bride and groom, it is a nice idea during the dinner to provide all the speakers with an A4 copy of this ORDER OF SPEECHES, printed on decorative paper.

Once they see their name in print, it tends to instantly focus them on the task at hand – if they are not already alerted. There is nothing worse than surprising someone who is not ready to speak – it makes everyone look very amateurish.

The order is insurance for the MC as well as the speakers – everyone knows what is going on and what is expected of them. As the MC is discussing the sequence, they should advise each speaker on microphone technique and lectern placement.

ORDER OF SPEECHES

Traditional

1 TOAST to the Bride & Groom proposed by

2 RESPONSE, and TOAST to the Bridal Party by the Groom/Bride

3 Response on behalf of the Bridal Party by the Best Man

4 Toast to the Bride's Parents by

5 Response by the Bride's Father

6 Toast to the Groom's Parents by

7 Response by the Groom's Father

8 Telegrams read by

Cutting of Cake

Bridal Waltz

Order of Speeches (European)

Father of the Bride

Father of the Groom

Best Man

The Groom

Explanation for the INTRODUCTION TO SPEECH TIME

For people who attend quite a few weddings, the speeches are what will distinguish one reception from another in terms of remembering the experience. You can have the same food, the same music and flowers, even the same guests, but there can never be the same words said in the same way.

The following speech has been written to help the MC change the energy in the room and the focus of the guests. As MC, you should try to memorise this speech – not word for word but idea for idea – and then say it in a way you feel is appropriate.

As you will notice from the MC's CHECKLIST, there are a number of different activities the MC must perform before starting the speeches, in order to help alter the energy and change the centre of attention. These are absolutely essential for a successful speech time.

In fact, I would go as far as to say that if the speeches are not successful (and there has been the proper prior consultation between the MC and bride and groom), then the MC must accept some responsibility for their failure.

Note: If the bride and groom have decided not to videotape their reception, advise them to at least have their speeches recorded; even if it is a friend standing at the back of the room with a camera on a tripod, they will appreciate your suggestion years later. Here, I speak from depressing personal experience.

INTRODUCTION TO SPEECH TIME

NB: It is very important to refer to the MC's CHECKLIST **before** you start.

Over the microphone, casually invite the guests to turn their seats to face the Bridal Table, to turn off their mobile phones, and to check if they have a glass in front of them for drinking a toast during the speeches. This will centre everyone's attention on what is about to happen and give them time to finish off their conversations. Once you are happy with everything, you can start by saying ....

They say a noisy crowd is a happy crowd – so you guys must be ecstatic!

I trust you have enjoyed your beautiful **meal** served so expertly by the staff here at .... If you have, then please join me in a round of applause, so the Chef can hear it (pause). Actually, I am just warming your hands up for what many people consider to be the highlight of the wedding reception; and that's the **speeches** – more so a highlight for the audience, rather than those people actually speaking! Some of the people you are about to hear, have never spoken in public before – so in consideration of that, let's please give our complete **attention** to them, and keep any children under control.

Well (B&G) .... it must be amazing to have all your friends and relations in one room at the same time. Did any of them happen to mention that the feast you've just experienced is often called the 'Wedding Breakfast'? Do you know why it is called the wedding breakfast? Because it's the first meal you have after you've *woken up* to what you've just done!

Traditionally, after the wedding breakfast is the time for us to pause and acknowledge what has actually happened here today, and pay respect to all of you who are involved in today's events.

(Today's date) .... signals a change and the start of a new relationship between two families. So it's only appropriate that we take time out now to reflect on the past and look towards the future; a future, which I might say, looks very bright for our beautiful bride and her handsome groom (he paid me extra to say that!).

But most important of all, we should acknowledge the marriage of (B&G) .... To start the proceedings, I would like to ask .... (refer to ORDER OF SPEECHES) to the microphone to propose a toast to the Bride & Groom. Please make welcome ....

You cannot force timing

Explanation of WEDDING FUNNIES

Unless you have a hysterically funny and well-rehearsed, original and scripted routine especially for weddings, it is better to let humour develop from what is going on around you. Be always on the lookout for unusual or interesting things that are happening and write them down. Comment on these aspects and move on, or keep them for when the opportunity arises. For instance, listen to the speeches and remember what someone has said in a fit of nerves.

I clearly remember the mileage I gained from a groom trying to explain the difference in attitudes concerning romance between the bride and himself by saying that '. . . my romance comes in spurts!' Or the best man who had trouble reading his notes because they were written in his wife's (the bride's sister Julie) tiny handwriting, announcing to the crowd that the bride has always been his 'favourite girl of the family'. I back-announced the best man by saying: *'That was Julie's ex-husband – giving a speech he will never forget – at least Julie will never let him forget it!'*

Take a look at the list of telegrams and jokes on the next page and note the ones that you personally find funny – they will be the jokes that suit your personality and that you can raise a laugh with. Learn one or two off by heart and have them ready to use, just in case the perfect chance arises. When and if the time comes, try to personalise the jokes for an even greater effect.

Each culture has it's own particular sense of what is funny and what is just downright disgusting and dirty. If you are unsure whether to use a joke because it might offend, then remember the MC's credo: 'If in doubt, then don't.' No-one will know what you did not say and this is not the most appropriate time to launch your career as a raunchy stand-up comedian.

Personally, I never use the 'marriage is a prison sentence' kind of humour. All the lines are very old, predictable and un-intelligent. The same goes for tacky mother-in-law jokes. Any MC who has developed their own style should not need to resort to such banal attempts to create amusement. Once the audience know you are going to tell boring 'gags', they will instantly label your service as a 'joke'.

Q: Why do lovers often hold hands?
A: They want to make sure that their rings don't fall off,
because they paid good money for them.

GAVIN, AGE 8

WEDDING FUNNIES

Telegrams

* From the (bride) to the (groom): DARLING, SINK INTO MY ARMS TONIGHT, 'CAUSE TOMORROW NIGHT YOUR ARMS WILL BE IN THE SINK!

* To the groom: CONGRATULATIONS .... ON MARRYING THE MOST BEAUTIFUL GIRL HERE TONIGHT. SHE IS A TALENTED, SENSITIVE, LOVING, UNDERSTANDING AND A SENSOUS WOMAN. FROM .... (the bride)

* To the groom: I'LL NEVER FORGET THOSE COLD, STORMY NIGHTS, THOSE LATE NIGHT RENDEZVOUS, AND ALL THOSE INTIMATE MOMENTS ONLY YOU AND I GOT TO SHARE – I'LL REMEMBER YOU FOREVER. REGARDS 'YOUR SINGLE BED'.

* To the groom: SORRY TO HEAR YOU ARE GETTING MARRIED TODAY – WE WILL ALWAYS LOVE YOU .... (groom) – FROM ALL YOUR FRIENDS AT TIFFANYS – WHERE MASSAGE IS AN ARTFORM.

* To the groom: LAUGH & THE WORLD LAUGHS WITH YOU – QUARREL WITH .... (the bride) AND YOU SLEEP ALONE.

* To the groom: CONGRATULATIONS FROM YOUR NEW IN-LAWS; HOWEVER BE WARNED – SHE LIKES TO SPEND MONEY, BUT THAT'S HER ONLY EXTRAVAGANCE! That's what she meant when she said 'Spend the rest of my life with you'.

* To the bride: CONGRATULATIONS (bride) YOU ARE A LUCKY, LUCKY WOMAN. TODAY YOU HAVE MARRIED A VERY SPECIAL MAN. BESIDES HIS QUICK-WITTED HUMOUR AND GRACIOUS MANNER, HE IS HUMBLE, KIND, GENEROUS AND THOUGHTFUL. THAT CUTE SMILE, THOSE SPARKLING EYES AND SOFT SUBTLE TOUCH . . . OHH, I COULD GO ON AND ON BUT THE BEST WOMAN HAS WON. WELL DONE AND BEST WISHES FROM YOUR NEW HUSBAND PETER.

* From the groom's football team: WE FOUND HIM TO BE USELESS IN EVERY POSITON. WE HOPE YOU (the bride) HAVE BETTER LUCK.

* To the groom: ON YOUR 18TH, YOU CELEBRATED IN BEER, ON

YOUR 21ST, YOU CELEBRATED IN WINE / RUM, ON YOUR WEDDING NIGHT, YOU CELEBRATED IN CIDER.

* IT HAS BEEN SAID THAT MARRIAGE IS A 50/50 PARTNERSHIP. I HOPE YOU REALISE THAT ANYONE WHO BELIEVES THIS KNOWS NOTHING ABOUT WOMEN AND FRACTIONS.

* DON'T SPRING ON THE INNER SPRING, 'CAUSE NEXT SPRING YOU'LL HAVE AN OFF SPRING!

* MAY YOU **NEVER** FORGET WHAT IS WORTH REMEMBERING OR REMEMBER WHAT IS BEST FORGOTTEN.

* MARRIAGE IS BUILT ON COMMUNICATION; BUT WHENEVER POSSIBLE, SAY WHAT YOU HAVE TO SAY DURING A COMMERCIAL.

* IT'S A WONDERFUL THING TO BE MARRIED. AS TIME GOES BY, YOU WAKE UP NEXT TO THAT PERSON EVERY DAY – TO HAVE THAT PERSON LOOK INTO YOUR EYES AND STILL SEE WHAT **YOU** THINK YOU LOOK LIKE.

* IT'S NEARLY TIME TO CONSUMATE YOUR VOWELS (sic). JUST REMEMBER – A STORK BRINGS A WHITE BABY, A RAVEN BRINGS A BLACK BABY, BUT A SWALLOW BRINGS NO BABY AT ALL.

One Liners

* A woman enjoys a man of strong will – as long as it's made out to her.

* My wife asked the priest if he believed in sex before marriage. The priest replied 'Not if it's going to make me late for the ceremony'.

* My wife said to me 'You're everything I want in a man'. I said 'And what's that?' She answered 'Not much!'

* Did you hear about the Irish bride & groom who sat up all night waiting for their sexual relations to arrive?

* Two TV antennas got married . . . the wedding was boring, but the reception was great!

* Society really needs children; they are essential to a marriage – how else do we program the videocassette or DVD recorder?

* The Father of the Bride said: 'It's not everyday that I give away a daughter, although there have been a few times when I've wanted to'.

* Marriage is like a game of noughts and crosses – when Julie is cross, Jim gets nought.

* The wife said, 'No, I don't wake up sleepy and irritable – I let him sleep in'.

* The husband said 'Our marriage is based on trust and understanding – she doesn't trust me, and I don't understand her'.

* I asked my wife what was on the TV – she said 'Dust'.

* She offered her honour, he honoured her offer and all night long it was honour and offer.

* My Daughter has not given us any trouble – as long as my wife and I did what we were told.

* The two most important words in a marriage are 'Yes Dear'.

* I overheard my wife asking her friends the other day 'What do you prefer – sex or cake?' Her friend asked 'What kind of cake?'

* There are 2 steps to a successful marriage: firstly, let your wife think she is having her own way and secondly, let her have her own way!

* I am not a 'yes' man to my wife – when she says 'no' I say 'no'.

* It's not who wears the pants that matters; it's how much money is in the pockets.

* The bride looks absolutely stunning – the groom looks absolutely stunned.

* The first time the groom set his eyes on the bride he was awe struck by her looks – to him, she was drop dead gorgeous. He said to her 'You're gorgeous' – and she said, 'Drop dead!'

* Remember: Marriage is the number one cause of divorce. It's TRUE! Statistically 100% of all divorces started with marriage!

* I married Miss Right. I just didn't know her first name was 'Always'.

* I haven't spoken to my wife for 18 months. I don't like to interrupt her.

* In the beginning, God created earth and rested. Then God created man and rested. Then God created woman. Since then, neither God nor man has rested.

* What is the difference between a dog and a fox? About 5 drinks.

* A beggar walked up to a well-dressed woman shopping in Toorak / Double Bay and said 'I haven't eaten anything in four days.' She looked at him and said, 'God, I wish I had your willpower'.

* Young Son asks: 'Dad, is it true; I heard that in some parts of Africa a man doesn't know his wife until he marries her?' Dad: 'That happens in every country, son'.

* To let a fool kiss you is stupid. To let a kiss fool you is worse.

* The most effective way to remember your wife's birthday is to forget it once.

* How do most men define marriage? An expensive way to get laundry done for free.

* Just think – if it weren't for marriage, men would go through life thinking they had no faults at all.

* If you want your wife to listen and pay undivided attention to every word you say, talk in your sleep.

* If love is blind, then why is lingerie so popular?

* A little boy asked his father, 'Daddy, how much does it cost to get married?' And the father replied, 'I don't know son, I'm still paying'.

* In an interview, Pamela Anderson said that if she were Hillary, she would have left President Clinton. In response, Clinton said, 'If Pamela Anderson was Hillary, none of this would have happened in the first place'.

* Father of the Bride: I was listening to Janet and Gary packing the car to go away the other day and they were fighting and squabbling. Y'know, a German philosopher once said: 'Man's morality is highest when in War'. Well, with that said, I think there's going to be a hell of a lot of morality in this marriage!

* 'Men are like a fine wine. They all start out like grapes and it's our job to stomp on them and keep them in the dark until they mature into something you'd like to have dinner with'. Author Unnamed

* 'The best way to get most husbands to do something is to suggest that perhaps they're too old to do it'. Ann Bancroft

* 'I think men who have a pierced ear are better prepared for marriage. They've experienced pain and bought jewellery'. Rita Rudner

* 'Keep your eyes wide open before marriage, half shut afterwards'. Benjamin Franklin

* 'A good wife always forgives her husband when she's wrong'. Milton Berle

* 'When women are depressed, they either eat or go shopping. Men invade another country. It's a whole different way of thinking'. Elaine Boosler

* 'The secret of a happy marriage remains a secret'. Henny Youngman

Wedding jokes

* The primary school teacher asked the students how many of the ten birds would be left on a branch if one were shot. 'None' said little Johnny 'because they would all fly away'. 'That's not quite the answer I was looking for little Johnny, but I like the way you're thinking,' said the teacher. Little Johnny reflects for a while then he says 'Teacher, if there are 3 women all eating an ice cream. One is licking it, the other one is sucking it and the last one is biting it, which one is married?' 'I guess the one that is sucking it' the teacher replies embarrassed. 'No' said little Johnny 'the one with the wedding ring on, but I like the way you're thinking'.

* The Greek groom said he was going to give his Australian bride something to remember, something she won't forget on their wedding night – something long and hard. His last name.

* When all the dead husbands arrived at the pearly gates, there was a sign saying, 'Please form two lines – one for hen-picked husbands and the other is for non hen-picked husbands'. Naturally the hen-picked line was full, so St Peter went up to the only guy in the non hen-picked husband line and asked why he was there when every one else was in the other line 'I don't know?' he shrugged his shoulders 'my wife told me to stand here'.

* The young son came home and proudly said he got a part in the new school drama production playing the role of a man who has been married for 20 years 'Congratulations' said his father 'next time you might get a speaking role'.

* After she woke up, a woman told her husband,' I just dreamed that you gave me a pearl necklace for St Valentine's Day. What do you think it means?' 'You'll find out on St Valentine's Day' he said. On St Valentine's Day, the man came home with a small package and gave it to his wife. Delighted, she opened it – to find a book entitled 'The Meaning of Dreams!'

AUDIENCE PARTICIPATION GAMES

Extra fun can be had from the guests using cutlery to tink the wine glasses. This noise cuts through most conversations and sends a message to all the other guests to join in. Soon there is a racket of metal against glass that keeps rising. As the call goes up, the bride and groom must cease what they are doing and kiss each other to stop the disturbance.

The MC might say: *'Hey, I just caught .... (the groom) tapping his own glass then!'*

A Danish tradition is if the groom leaves the reception for any reason, any of the males in the room can sneak a kiss on the cheek of the bride; and vice versa.

There are other versions of this game that involve the bride and groom (and / or the bridal party) singing a song or reciting a poem, as the glasses are tinked. The rules for this must be established immediately preceding the first occasion when the bride and groom kiss. Alternatively, Joel Sweeney suggests that an MC might announce '. . . from now on, the bride and groom will only kiss when a song is sung with the word love in it' – or some other agreed cue.

During the speeches, the MC can ask the bride and groom to stand up. The bride puts her right arm out straight and the groom follows by placing his outstretched arm on top of the bride's. The MC can then announce: *'Ladies and gentlemen, this is the last time you will ever see .... (the groom) have the upper hand in this relationship!'*

And still more: 'Throwing the Fish' involves everyone in a circle with the bride and groom in the middle. Whoever catches the toy fish has to speak for thirty seconds about the couple. Otherwise, you can blindfold the groom and ask him to recognise the bride by kissing all the ladies on the cheek or blindfolding the bride and cajoling her into feeling the hands of the men assembled in the circle. The penalty for an incorrect answer could be a drink, a jig or push-ups.

Explanation of *The Keys*

This is a fun group participation activity that is set up by the MC. It was origi-nally a practical joke played on the bride, which unfortunately gave the wrong impression to some of the guests. I consider the bride to be unassailable on her wedding day, but anyone can 'pay out' the groom.

You need to recruit ladies of all ages (and some extrovert men!) from the audi-ence, plus about 10 to 15 old keys supplied by the MC. Approach the selected guests just before the speeches begin – it is wise to choose outgoing personali-ties. Ask them to do you a 'favour' by being part of a practical joke to be played on the groom later. When they agree, heighten the secrecy by sliding a key next to their plate; everyone else at the table will wonder what is going on and want a piece of the action. The participants seem to enjoy it more if they are part of a group, so look for an opportunity to involve the whole table.

The best time to insert this game is usually at the end of the speeches, before or after the reading of the telegrams.

As soon as the dialogue has been read out (see template) – or memorised and spoken – instruct the DJ to loudly play the opening bars of 'Another One Bites the Dust' by Queen or 'To All The Girls I've Loved Before' by Willie Nelson and Julio Iglesias. This will prompt the participants, one by one, to leave their seats and march triumphantly towards the bridal table, dropping the key in the groom's lap with a flirtatious wink.

This piece of fun is much more suited to the modern groom, especially if he is slightly reserved as a person. Depending upon the groom's sense of humour, it is generally accepted well by everyone concerned. Also, you can see him thinking, after all the 10 to 15 keys are returned, saying to himself 'Wow – I wish I had been this lucky!'

The MC could finish by saying, *'Hmm, you've got a bit of explaining to do.'*

The Keys

Now we all know (the groom) .... as a quiet and unassuming sort of character / bloke.

Is this correct? (Pause) Well 'Absolutely not!' according to some of his long-term friends. This mild-mannered facade we all recognise is apparently a complete smokescreen. Like all mild sea breezes, they can often hide a real hurricane lurking just around the corner; and that is just what we have here with .... (the groom).

Many of you might not know this, but .... was known at (insert actual name of the High school the groom attended) as 'Casanova' and had nicknames like .... (e.g. Jumpin' Jones) to his credit. It's true! This information comes to me from very reliable sources!

But now that he has gone from a single to a married man .... feels a little embarrassed about this outrageous past when he was a true 'Party Animal'. So he has asked me to do him a little favour; to set the record straight, as it were.

Without making it too obvious – all this is highly confidential you realise, (so keep it amongst yourselves) .... has requested that all the ladies – and whoever else – he has ever given his front door or even bedroom key to, could they please now bring them up to the front and return them, without too much fuss – so as not to embarrass (the bride) .... too much.

Come on up now, own up .... but please make it quick!

(Music starts with the volume taking precedence.)

The Love Shoe Game

This game makes an excellent alternative to the reading of bad taste fictitious 'telegrams'. It is meant to test how well-suited the bride and groom are to each other and give them an idea of how well they know each other.

Although the MC can host the Love Shoe Game, it is best if someone who is close to the bride and groom, such as a groomsmen or a bridesmaid do the honours due to the personal nature of the questions. The MC can set it up and organise the chairs to be brought out on cue.

After the last speech, and before the wedding cake is cut (when telegrams are usually read) is the best time to play the Love Shoe Game. The MC makes an announcement: *'Ladies and gentlemen, I ask you to welcome the bride's sister CHERYL up to the lectern for some important wedding business'*. (The bride and groom are now scratching their heads and looking puzzled.)

CHERYL 'Since JOHN & SUE will be spending the rest of their lives together after tonight, the Bridal Party have decided that it might be worthwhile to see how compatible JOHN & SUE actually are. Therefore we have put together a little test that will gauge to what extent this match has been made in heaven.'

(This is the cue for the MC and a reliable staff member on the opposite side of the floor to simultaneously bring a chair each out in the middle of the floor in front of the bridal table and place them together back to back.)

CHERYL *'Now JOHN & SUE if you would please take a seat'* (The bride & groom make their way onto the dance floor and sit down – back to back; completely confused.)

CHERYL 'JOHN & SUE will you please take off your shoes.' (They do so.)

'Now JOHN please give SUE one of your shoes and SUE give JOHN one of yours.' (They do so.)

'JOHN & SUE please listen carefully. I am going to ask you a series of questions relating to courtship and married life. To answer each question you both simply raise high into the air the shoe of who you think the answer applies to. You must raise only one shoe at a time and you must not turn around to look. Are you ready?'

Some examples of questions:

1 On the day you first met who first made eye contact and began to flirt, JOHN or SUE?

2 On the first date who made the most effort to impress, JOHN or SUE?

3 After one month who was the keener of the two, JOHN or SUE?

4 After six months who was the keener of the two, JOHN or SUE?

5 Who first hinted about marriage, JOHN or SUE?

6 Who was the most enthusiastic about making all these wedding arrangements, JOHN or SUE?

7 Who is the best cook, JOHN or SUE?

8 Who is more likely to want to go and eat out in a restaurant, JOHN or SUE?

9 Who is more likely to pay when you eat out in a restaurant, JOHN or SUE?

10 Who takes the longest to get ready when you go out, JOHN or SUE?

11 Who is more likely to leave dirty dishes in the sink, JOHN or SUE?

12 Who is more likely to leave a dirty sock on the floor, JOHN or SUE?

13 Who is more likely to make the bed, JOHN or SUE?

14 Who is more likely to take out the rubbish bins, JOHN or SUE?

15 Who is more likely to control the TV remote control, JOHN or SUE?

16 Who is more likely to control the lounge, JOHN or SUE?

17 Who is more likely to want a late night chocolate fix, JOHN or SUE?

18 Who becomes more 'clucky' around children, JOHN or SUE?

19 Who will be the first to say 'I want a baby', JOHN or SUE?

20 Who will then be the first to say 'Let's start practicing tonight', JOHN or SUE?

Conclusion: After all the questions, the host announces 'The results of this test mean the following . . .'

(0–5): HMMMM. Good luck.

(6–0): A few surprises are awaiting you.

(11–15): You are both very compatible.

(16–20): This is a match made in heaven.

'JOHN & SUE your score was 17 out of 20 so this is indeed a match made in heaven.'

Explanation of the INTERVIEW

An MC needs to give the impression to the assembled guests that he or she is on a par with them as far as their relationship with the bride and groom goes. One way to guarantee this happens is to conduct an 'interview' with the bride and groom beforehand.

All this personal information can be gathered during the consultation two weeks prior to the day, when the WEDDING PARTY DETAILS and RECEPTION PROCEDURE sheets have already been completed and are then discussed and confirmed. It is a good idea to ask the bride and groom to bring along a copy of their wedding invitation, which will give the MC an idea of the theme and style of the wedding reception they have planned.

The stories, facts and figures the MC collects on the INTERVIEW page are then used as an adjunct to the information that has already been revealed about the bride and groom by the previous speakers during the event.

If the groom chooses not to use the story of their engagement or courtship (refer to '5 easy rules for preparing a wedding speech') it is of great value (and humour) for the guests to hear about how the two got together. It is best to leave this story to last in case one of the other speakers (or the groom) has decided to use it.

In some cases, where the wedding proposal was awkward, I have used my acting skills to imitate the scene of the groom's embarrassing or inept attempt at romance. Given the right scenario, this vignette can 'bring the house down'.

The INTERVIEW

Bride
Where did you grow up?

Where do you work?

Groom
Where did you grow up?

Works at?

Interests / Sports?

During the relationship
Where, how & when did you meet?

How did he propose?

Are there any memorable incidents during the courtship?

Which hotel are you going to after the reception?

Where is the honeymoon?

General
Are there any relatives that need special mentioning e.g. the cake maker?

Grandparents' recent wedding anniversaries?

People who have travelled a long way?

Master of ceremonies
Will I have my meal with the guests during the reception?

Is there easy parking at the venue?

Can we fix up final payment now please?

Index

Bibliography

'The Wedding MC Handbook' by Joel Sweeney, DTM
'The Complete Guide to Wedding Speeches' by John Haslem

Author's background

Peter L. Miller started his working life as an actor on Australian television shows and international musicals after completing his training at the Drama Studio, Sydney.

While still acting, Peter found that his skills were helpful to others outside the sphere of drama. He began teaching presentation techniques to executives who had been cast in their company's corporate videos or required to speak at the industry conference. Today he coaches and writes about public speaking while still performing as a corporate Master of Ceremonies, compere, and presenter.

He is the director A WEDDING MC HOTLINE. This business mainly hires actors and specialises in providing first-class multi-lingual Masters of Ceremonies for every kind of wedding to every major venue around Australia.

He is the author of UP FRONT IN CONTROL, 5 EASY STEPS TO A FANTASTIC VOICE, YOU CAN BE A WEDDING MC, and PRESENTATION EXCELLENCE.

A NIGHT IN THE LIFE OF A WEDDING MC

Everybody has attended weddings where the Master of Ceremonies ruined what was potentially a great occasion.

Replace this unfortunate scenario with the spontaneity, charm, humour and class of a professional Master of Ceremonies. Fully prepared and excited to be there. Communication skills beyond what most people imagine being adequate.

A specialised wedding MC knows exactly what is expected of him. He has impeccable manners, is punctual, well-dressed, articulate, and tactful. Experience has given him the ability to handle a variety of people and to always be appropriate and sensitive to particular customs, traditions and cultures.

The professional Master of Ceremony at a wedding is a unique individual with a high self-esteem and yet is modest enough to let all the attention shine on the bride and groom; not himself.

Over the cordless microphone (that he may have supplied), he welcomes everyone to the venue and proceeds to change the atmosphere from a spiritual one to a *party place* where Celebration is the name of the game. He warms up the audience for what is about to happen.

Confidently, he introduces the parents and the bridal party and then makes a huge song and dance about the entrance of the guests of honour for the day – the bride & groom. The guests immediately sense that they are in the hands of someone who knows exactly what he's doing and instantly relax.

After things have settled down slightly, guests share a 'feast', quaffed down with alcohol; none of which touches the lips of our professional MC. He then rises to introduce the speakers; all of whom have been properly prepared by the MC himself – weeks before the event. They have used the sample speeches he has supplied to write down and practise some words of wisdom that are sincere and heartfelt. This is the emotional highpoint of the evening.

Tears are shed amongst the gathering but no-one is embarrassed because all the words were said with honesty and poise – the MC made sure of that with his helpful wedding speech guide given out beforehand.

There was none of the usual nervousness or attempt at humour that everyone has come to expect from wedding speakers; and none of the regret felt by the speaker after they have sat down and realised there was so much more they wanted to say.

Experience takes over now and the MC really comes into his own with quick, witty responses that everyone understands and enjoys immensely. The wedding reception now has a life of its own – everyone is high on the energy in the room.

The MC has enticed the guests to get involved with their cameras and well wishes and to raise a glass of champers and toast to the long & happy life of our bride and groom.

The world's newest husband and wife are asked to cut their traditional wedding cake together, and then invited to dance their first romantic dance as Mr & Mrs. Everyone starts to loosen up as the MC prompts the entire group to get involved on the dance floor and let go of any inhibitions; leading to the well-staged throwing of the bouquet, the catching of the garter, the farewell circle and the guard of honour. All performed with high entertainment value.

He brings the night to its natural peak as the couple then exit from the room and towards their 'get away' car. The MC has already ensured that their luggage has been safely deposited inside the boot of the limousine and organised all their valuable gifts to be stored safely away while on honeymoon.

All that needs now is for the professional Master of Ceremonies to elegantly close the evening and gather everyone together once more to wish them farewell.

Everyone knows they have attended a magnificent occasion; but they are not sure what was the best part! All they know is that everything fitted together beautifully, the event flowed well, and there were no boring gaps. It was an experience most will never forget.

The Master of Ceremonies packs up his briefcase and smiles as he bids 'goodnight' to the staff who again welcomed him as part of their team. He drives home exhausted but satisfied that he has contributed to another successful celebration of love.

The lesson here is to choose your MC carefully – you only get one chance to get it right on the night.

These are the kind of comments you should look for when hiring your MC:

'We believe it was one of the best decisions we made in co-coordinating & planning our day. We had no concerns about how smoothly the reception would run. The time you spent with us prior to the day proved invaluable. Your professionalism, friendliness and humour worked well with us and our guests! Thanks Peter, we had a great night.' **Diana & Jason Caravana, Sebel Spa & Resort, Windsor.**

'Just a note to thank you for your superb MC performance at our wedding. Everyone would like to thank you for helping them during their hour of need. Especially Trevor, who has said you were 'fantastic'!! Thanks for everything and we hope that you enjoyed the night as well.' **Julie and Trevor Martin, Curzon Hall.**

(This is an article that appeared in the May 2003 edition of WEDDING STYLE AUSTRALIA magazine. It is available as an Adobe Acrobat file from www.weddingmc.com.au)

SPEAKERS LOVE WORDS – HERE'S ONE TO ADD TO YOUR VOCABULARY

Explaining the meaning of word 'Compere' to Americans
by Peter L. Miller, Australia

You wouldn't be in the business of speaking if you didn't love words.

Its impossible to accurately say how many words we each know as individuals (scrabble players aside!). Well here's a new word that might come in handy as a speaker because it defines what some of us do a little clearer. The word is 'Compere', pronounced the same as 'compare'.

A compere is a different version of what Americans call an emcee or MC.

Many other western nations use the word compere to distinguish between the different roles each person plays when they are *up front and in control.* The term compere is of French origin meaning godfather and is adapted from the word conferencier.

Am I an MC or a compere?

The *Oxford* Dictionary is no help on this one – it gives the same definition for each word. Semantics aside, a compere is someone who is running the entire show or event, the focal point, a solo performer; an entertainer without being musical. A compere will take an audience from one situation to the next and be totally involved in all of it. A compere is there for the whole time, 'hands on', always commenting on the action on stage and building a real dynamic relationship with the audience in the process. If something is happening on stage, then the compere will be involved somehow. If nothing is happening, then the compere is also 'not happening' and some music will probably be playing.

Both an MC and compere have a responsibility to link the audience with the action on stage. The skills are the same for each role, but as I point out in Chapter 6 of UP FRONT IN CONTROL, the preparation and responsibilities are not the same because the *objectives* are distinctly different.

Instead of being totally involved in all the action on stage, the MC will get the show started, and then move on and off the stage, introducing, announcing, commenting and housekeeping. An MC will *share* the lectern with a lot more people than a compere will.

Comperes and MCs serve different functions in the marketing campaign of a product launch. A compere will be required where there is more audience interaction and flexibility and also less formality.

Where the dialogue is less structured and the run sheet more adaptable (given that the amount of audience interaction is difficult to pin down precisely from a time point of view), comperes are defined by their ability to speak spontaneously and without notes. This flexibility naturally creates a less ceremonial atmosphere.

In Australia, many speakers extend their income base by using the skills they already possess by working as the Master of Ceremony for the convention they are also speaking at. Emceeing is one of the real growth areas of the speaking industry; promoted by the book 'UP FRONT IN CONTROL – Great MC's reveal their trade secrets'.

tion *noun*, **compensatory** *adjective*

compère (*say* **kom**-pair) *noun* a person who introduces the performers in a show or broadcast. **compère** *verb* [French, = godfather]

compete *verb* (**competed, competing**) take part in a competition.

(This is an article that appeared in the Summer 2001 Vol. 23 Issue 5 edition of SHARING IDEAS magazine. It is available as an Adobe Acrobat file from www.compere.com.au)

The great cartoons in this book are drawn by my friend and international award winning cartoonist Mr Tony (A.J.) Kentuck.

Tony was born in London, raised in Wales and started cartooning in the British Army. He then travelled to Australia to further his cartooning ambitions and worked as editorial cartoonist for The Sunday Times and community newspapers group in Perth. Tony now lives on the northern beaches of Sydney and works from a studio in Brookvale.

Visit the website www.rmdad.com.au to view more of the famous Kentuck Collection. This wonderful series includes a Legal, Medical, Music, Golf, Chiropractic, Real Estate and Gym series of very funny colour cartoons for your office wall or as a surprise gift for that special client.

Tony also is a popular convention and trade show personality. His quick cartoon caricatures and on-the-spot illustrations of anybody (who can stay still for 5 minutes) are a sure-fire attraction to the booth of the company he is working for.

Contact Tony ajkentuck@optusnet.com.au

Guaranteed to make you into a star speaker - get a hold of the

WONDERFUL WEDDING SAMPLE SPEECHES

Forget those tired quotes from the Internet that are in everyone's speech.
Forget the imported paperback 'guides' that you'll find in any bookshop.
Forget those boring, out-dated and old-fashioned speeches.

Get up-to-date. Get local and be original.

These are modern word-for-word speeches that are easy to use and really work to make you look like a champion speaker.

Taken from the very best <u>genuine</u> speeches that the author has heard from being the MC at over 1,000 weddings.

This easy-to-read document consists of sample speeches for the entire bridal party and parents including the groom, the bride, both fathers, and

the best man. You can learn the "5 easy rules to preparing a wedding speech" (including the famous ZIG ZAG method), know the crucial do's & dont's and get suggestions on how to raise a toast. It even includes advice on what to say about anyone who has been recently deceased.

Besides all this, there are tips and hints on how to devise, construct and deliver an original, heartfelt and sincere speech that you will be proud of. You can take your seat and say to yourself 'I nailed that!'

Available from www.compere.com.au

Photos by Alan Kan 04111 766 22 alankhan.com

Every wedding should be an entirely stress-free affair. With this unique book, it will be.

Written by 'MC of the Year' Peter L. Miller, this easy-to-use manual gives you:

- Word for word introductions, announcements & toasts

- A tasteful selection of one-liners & telegrams

- 5 easy steps to writing a great wedding speech

- Audience games

- Checklists, run sheets and much, much more

There is even advice on fees & how to source work as an MC & Compere plus acting techniques to help deal with nerves

Peter Miller's method is used by all the leading MCs across the world to help everyone involved be thoroughly organised and still really enjoy the event.

This structure gives MCs a chance to be spontaneous and react instinctively to what is going on around them.

Filled with great cartoons, diagrams and written in a entertaining manner, this book will make anyone a confident, professional looking and sounding Master of Ceremonies.

Available from www.weddingmc.com.au

An early attempt at marketing my services:

Host a Murder-
kill off Uncle Harry!

A WEDDING MC HOTLINE is very proud of the excellent reputation we have as a leader in the wedding industry. We are the first company to successfully put an end to using old 'Uncle Harry'.

THE PAST

The business started as "Peter Miller Entertainment Services" more than 14 years ago to serve the entertainment needs of the discriminating bride and groom. Gradually moving from supplying MCs, disc jockeys, singers as well as lighting and sound equipment, Peter L. Miller decided it was more beneficial to offer each couple the single Master of Ceremony service and let the other entertainment agencies handle the rest. However, that single service had to be the very best and absolutely '1st Class'.

Earn $$$ from
a Wedding Master of Ceremony Agency

THE PRESENT

These days, we are Australia's leading agency for MC's - winner of "MC of the Year" in 1998 and qualifying as a finalist in the recent Suncorp Parramatta Regional Awards for Business Excellence. When you hire an MC from 'A WEDDING MC HOTLINE' you are getting the finest there is. No other MC service comes close to our attention to detail plus the experience and advice that comes included with your investment.

THE FUTURE

Everywhere, right throughout the world, people will continue to fall in love and get married. Weddings are a wonderful environment to work in and what could be better than helping to organise an event based on love? We will show you how it's done. A total business system is available for each market to take advantage of this wonderful opportunity and create a passive income stream. With very little capital outlay and by following our proven structure, you can grow a business and bring joy to yourself, your family and your community.

**Freecall 1800 888 062 to discuss how
to get rid of Uncle Harry**

www.abia.com.au

Hi there – I'm the Corporate Compere. I guarantee to make your next special event entertaining, informative and on- time

Your corporate function ...

As your MC, Peter L. Miller will set a professional atmosphere with a feeling of motivation, inspiration, excitement and energy.

Whether your event is a Conference, Award night, Trade show, or Product launch, A CORPORATE COMPERE will ensure that your meeting runs smoothly.

Peter's style is

- Humorous - A self-deprecating dry Aussie sense of comedy that does not offend
- Friendly '...we're here to do some work - but let's have a good time while we do it'
- Flexible – from introducing the CEO to drawing the raffle
- Professional – thoroughly prepared & researched so that everyone thinks he is part of the company
- Intelligent – knows what, when & where is appropriate

Over 500 of the worlds leading corporations have trusted

Peter L. Miller to be their Master of Ceremonies. Some of these companies include: Samsung. Mitsubishi. Macquarie Bank. Polaroid. MBF. Tandy. Komatsu. Atlas Copco, Master Foods. HOYTS. NuSkin. SmithKline Beecham, CleverLink, AVID and Citibank. Peter was awarded the 'MC of the Year' in 1998 (ABJA)

Special Skills that will enlighten your event include:

- Interviewing and Facilitation
- Singing customised lyrics dedicated to celebrating the event
- A Keynote address or workshop on "Selling Is Communication"
- Audience games, quizzes, team activities
- Designing a run sheet or agenda

For details on how to book
the CORPORATE COMPERE, go to www.compere.com.au

Expand your talent with

UP FRONT IN CONTROL

How to be the perfect Master of Ceremonies for any business or social event
by Peter L. Miller & Ron Tacchi

This book is a hands-on, how to manual that took more than 7 years to write. The 180 pages draw on more than 30 years combined experience with audiences from around the world.

It contains secrets, short cuts, procedures & checklists that will guarantee your next assignment will be better prepared and more rewarding for you & your audience. It has everything and anything you will need to know in order to succeed *'up front'* with an audience.

PLUS the book shows you how to add a further income stream to your speaking activities and add value to your marketing portfolio.

Experienced masters of ceremony reveal their trade secrets
for the very first time ever

Topics covered in this edition are:

- How to use humour
- How to deal with hecklers
- The fine line between a speaker, entertainer & MC
- Acting techniques to make you calm & cool, on & off stage
- What's the difference between a Compere and an MC?
- Personal style incl. grooming, fancy dress & your voice
- Marketing your services as a professional MC
- Acknowledgments & thank yous
- How to design a runsheet
- Introducing speakers, proposing a toast, presenting gifts
- Corporate events
- Award nights
- Outdoor events, fashion parades, retail promotions

For MC's, Presenters, Compere's & Hosts

UP FRONT
IN CONTROL

Trade Secrets Revealed For The First Time

PLUS grab the 90 minute CD interview with both authors. It is hysterically funny and covers some topics from the book in a more in-depth perspective + new subjects not covered in the book such as the rise of female MC's.

Available from www.compere.com.au

One-to-one Coaching

PRESENTATION EXCELLENCE

Imagine...

Your audience are on the edge of their seats; hanging on your every word; laughing and learning from you.

This is possible. The secrets of live corporate communication all originate from the Theatre. Using basic acting techniques that excite your audience, Peter L. Miller has developed an extremely easy but effective coaching program.

Using the famous 'Fishbone Technique' we will together create a powerful presentation that gives you leverage with its flexible format.

At the end of only 4 sessions, you will have a portable, entertaining and unique talk that you can perform at anytime, anywhere with almost any group - be they business, social or industry specific.

Peter L. Miller will help you to

- **captivate** an audience's attention
- **connect** each person to your message
- **encourage** the participants to contribute
- **sell** much, much more than you ever have

Invest in one-on-one coaching and **awaken the speaker within** - you will dramatically improve yourself and your chances of success. Why not jump ahead a few rungs of the ladder and get to the top quicker - it's not so crowded up there!

Enquire at **www.presentationexcellence.com.au**

PRESENTATION EXCELLENCE

The E-Book

Some direct quotes from the text:

- There are few better ways to **leverage** your **time** and **message** than to speak in public.

- It is ironic, but both repetition and brevity are the presenter's most powerful allies.

$$E + P = R$$
Experience + **P**reparation = **R**esult

- Your intention as a speaker is to be yourself on stage and carry a **genuine**, **sincere**, and **happy-to-be-there** confidence; a natural extension of your own personality.

- You should strive to be **memorable**. The best way to do this is to make your audience aware of something new - to **improve their focus**.

- An audience will appreciate it if you endeavour to reach them through their **hearts** and not their **heads**

- Inspire your audience to ask themselves how they **feel** about what you are saying.

If these words are making sense to you, then maybe it's time to build on what you already know and add the parts that are missing. You can print out the 70 pages or read it off your screen.

Take yourself to the next level - take your career to where you know you should be. Realise your potential as a first rate communicator and order the e-book now from...

www.presentationexcellence.com.au

VOCAL HYGIENE

3 WAYS TO KEEP THE VOICE HAPPY, HEALTHY AND WORKING TO MAXIMUM POTENTIAL

1 The Tongue Scraper

The toothbrush is for the teeth, dental floss is for the gums, and scraping is for the tongue. The morning ritual of tongue scraping has been used in many Asian countries for centuries. This is a fascinating and unique health accessory – especially for speakers & singers. Tongue scraping is known to prevent sore throats, coughs, and colds and help the vocal apparatus to remain healthy & hygienic by removing the debris that gather on our tongue while we sleep.

2 Ginseng & Royal Jelly

Many staples of Oriental medicine derive from the amazing root called Ginseng. After you have scraped your tongue, protect the vocal cords with this brilliant combination of tonics and honey. It coats the vocal cords and protects them in the process. The ginseng by-products all have recuperative, strengthening and invigorating qualities.

(Asthmatics are warned off from using this method as the veneers can sometimes make the breathing hole a bit smaller.)

3 Ginger Tea

Another rudimentary ingredient of any good Chinese kitchen is the delicious beverage made from the ginger root. Mixed with hot water & drunk like tea, this naturally soothes any sore or damaged parts of the vocal apparatus. It is particularly helpful to properly digest food, which in turn makes the stomach settle and produce clean, clear & consistent breath.

ORDER FOR YOUR WELL BEING FROM WWW.COMPERE.C.AU

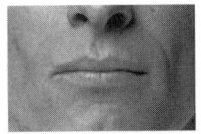

YOU ARE GUARANTEED A FANTASTIC VOICE!

in just 21 days

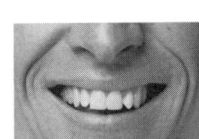

Influence people now - with the power of your voice!

WHAT YOU'LL LEARN...

- The secrets that give you the clear, strong, attractive voice you've always wanted.

- How to eliminate unpleasant sounds or accents and prevent sore throats.

- Discover your own natural <u>singing</u> voice.

- How to warm-up your voice and keep it sounding great.

THE METHODS ARE SIMPLE AND AMAZINGLY EFFECTIVE

Hi there, I work as a Professional Voice Coach, Actor and Corporate MC.

With my program '5 EASY STEPS TO A FANTASTIC VOICE', I've developed the voice potential of famous TV presenters, radio stars and professional speakers.

Now with this audio and video set, I will be your own personal voice coach. Take your voice to the gym.

5 EASY STEPS TO A FANTASTIC VOICE is a straightforward voice improvement programme available in many formats.

For your EARS, choose either the CD or cassette.
For your EYES, watch how the experts do it (and become an expert yourself) then get the video or CD-rom and the ebook.

This recording also offers encouragement and advice on how to sing with ease, and control nerves when speaking in public. These are essential Life Skills.

Testimonials
"As a professional speaker and speech coach, Peter L. Miller's 5 EASY STEPS TO A FANTASTIC VOICE is an invaluable tool for me". **Patricia Fripp, CSP, CPAE, Past President, National Speakers Assoc. USA**

For speakers and singers
5 EASY STEPS TO A FANTASTIC VOICE

How to influence people by the way you speak
by Peter Miller

www.compere.com.au

Your specialist online wedding store

Newlywed.com.au is an online wedding store offering a large range of products, including:

- **Newlywed Name Change Kits**
- Stunning ostrich feather quill pens in a range of colours
- DIY Cristina Re invitation stationery & wedding favours
- Hair diamonds
- Blubells wedding software
- Winston & Albert Ring Bear-ers
- Bridal accessories, garters & ring pillows
- Legal Will Kits
- Wedding books
- Bridal files - for the organised bride

www.newlywed.com.au

Monthly competitions, helpful articles, secure online ordering

As seen in Bride To Be & Complete Wedding Magazines

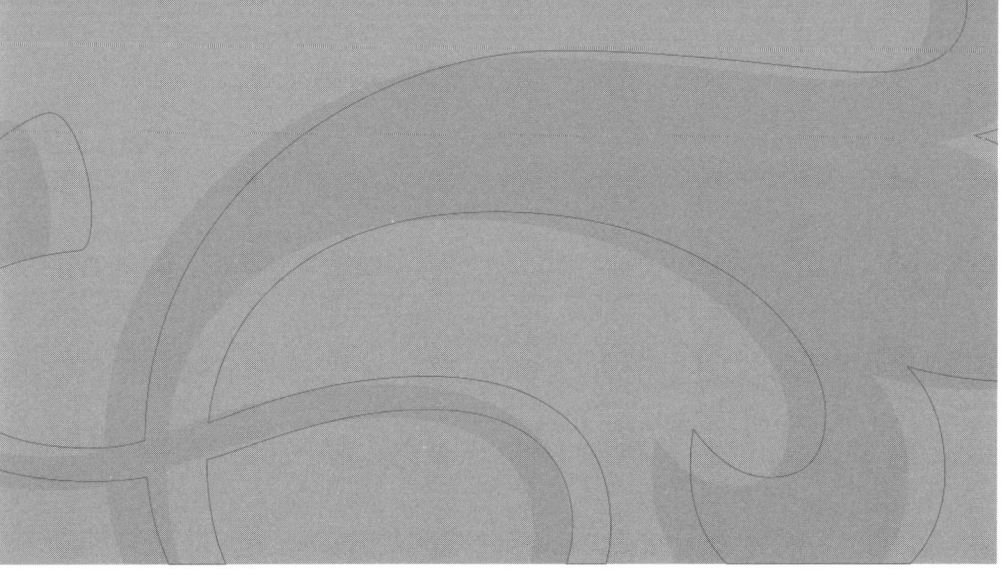

Advance your
Master of Ceremonies career
and professionalism . . .

Extend the value of this book by acquiring the entire list of 15 helpful templates via email. They will be deposited instantly to your 'Inbox' as a (virus-free) M/S WORD attachment so you can manipulate them any way you like.

There is no photocopying or scanning needed – you can personalise each template to your own (or clients') specifications. This equals hundreds of hours saved and gives you a ready-made manual to jumpstart your MC and Compere business straight away.

Weddings:

MC's CHECKLIST
WEDDING PARTY DETAILS
RECEPTION PROCEDURE
MC's OPENING SPEECH
INTRODUCTION TO SPEECHTIME
ORDER OF SPEECHES
AUDIENCE PARTICIPATION GAMES
THE INTERVIEW
WEDDING FUNNIES

Corporate:

SAMPLE RUN SHEET
BRIEFING QUESTIONS
BUSINESS MC's CHECKLIST
SPEAKERS' CHECKLIST
MC's PRE-FUNCTION QUESTIONNAIRE
ENQUIRY FORM
FEEDBACK FORM
GENERIC CONTRACT

Available from www.compere.com.au

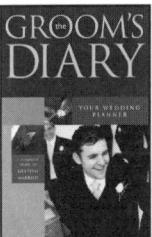